The Urbana Free Library

To renew materials call
217-367-4057

The Pedant's Return

The Pedant's Return

Why the Things You Think Are Wrong Are Right

Andrea
Barham

BANTAM BOOKS / NEW YORK

15⁰⁰

THE PEDANT'S RETURN
A Bantam Book

PUBLISHING HISTORY
Michael O'Mara Books UK hardcover edition published 2006
Bantam Books hardcover edition / September 2007

Published by
Bantam Dell
A Division of Random House, Inc.
New York, New York

Book design by Susan Turner

Library of Congress Cataloging-in-Publication Data
Barham, Andrea.
The pedant's return: why the things you think are wrong are right / Andrea
Barham.
p. cm.
Includes bibliographical references.
ISBN: 978-0-553-38491-8 (hardcover)
1. Common fallacies. 2. Handbooks, vade-mecums, etc. I. Title.

AZ999.B28 2007
001.9'6—dc22
2007014806

Printed in the United States of America
Published simultaneously in Canada

www.bantamdell.com

10 9 8 7 6 5 4 3 2 1
BVG

For Great-Aunt Rose

*To become properly acquainted with a truth,
we must first have disbelieved it, and disputed against it.*

NOVALIS
(Friedrich Leopold, Baron von Hardenberg)

Contents

Acknowledgments

ANDY BARHAM, ANDY JERRISON, AND SIMON BLACKMAN HAVE CONTINued in their loveliness. Margaret Crawley was most helpful in her proofreading. Thank you to all the experts who kindly corroborated my fanciful-sounding findings. I am also most grateful to my editor, Helen Cumberbatch, who is as thoughtful as she is thorough. Thank you also to the team at Michael O'Mara Books for being so delightful.

One small confession: I still appear to have Jennifer Blackman's chair, which I borrowed in an emergency capacity some considerable time ago. Ssh!

Foreword

THE PEDANT RETURNS WITH FURTHER CORRECTIONS. THIS VOLUME IS a collection of preposterous-sounding assertions that all turned out to be entirely correct. I have looked into a wealth of entirely implausible-sounding claims and discovered the truth behind them. The Pilgrims really did land prematurely at Plymouth Rock because they had run out of beer. Eating undercooked kidney beans, apple seeds, and green potatoes can prove fatal. And there really was an Irish Bible that exhorted its readers to "sin on more."

Facts can be fun, but when they appear—as they so often do—unexplained and uncorroborated, it is impossible to judge their accuracy. Yet, there is no need for this dearth of substantiation. To paraphrase Churchill, nowadays, never has so much information been available to so many for so little outlay: Copious amounts of reliable information are electronically available to all (who have a library card) via the library's on-line reference service. Quiz your librarian about home access to the *Encyclopaedia Britannica* and other great works of reference. Or better yet, read this book, since I've done all the looking-up for you.

While doing so, I found that it was often the background information that proved to be the most fascinating part. Possibly, you are aware that Virginia Woolf wrote all her books standing up, but do you know why? Many truths revealed interesting associated stories: Mozart was buried in a mass grave and Einstein did badly at school—but neither of these things happened for the reasons one might expect.

The final chapter is, to my mind, the most interesting since it contains a collection of falsely discredited facts. Cinderella should never have had her glass slippers relegated to fur; chop suey should never have had its origins transferred to the United States, and would-be know-it-alls should never have boasted that glass was a liquid! All the entries in this category are cases of impressive-sounding-theory-but-wrong syndrome. That said, all current theories are, of course, just best guesses made from the information we have to hand. We're only human, after all....

ANDREA BARHAM
August 2006

CHAPTER 1

Art *and* Literature

PLAYWRIGHT WILLIAM SHAKESPEARE STOLE HIS PLOTLINES

THE TRADESMAN'S SON WHO, IN 1578, LEFT SCHOOL AT THE AGE OF fourteen and who married at eighteen (after getting a local girl pregnant) is nowadays regarded as the greatest dramatist of all time. Therefore, as Andrew Dickson writing in *The Rough Guide to Shakespeare* says, "It can be a surprise to learn how much Shakespeare depended on sources and allegories for his plays and poems." John Michell, author of *Who Wrote Shakespeare?*, tells us that Shakespearean scholars have always admitted that "Shakespeare borrowed freely from contemporary as well as ancient authors." Said contemporaries of the up-and-coming playwright also noticed this tendency to borrow. One such was Ben Jonson, whom the *Encyclopaedia Britannica* describes as the "second most important English dramatist" of the time. Jonson authored an epigram called *On Poet-Ape* that tells of a fellow writer who "would pick and glean, / Buy the reversion of old plays, now grown / To a little wealth, and credit on the scene." Jonson goes on to complain that this unnamed offender "takes up all, makes each man's wit his own, / And told of this, he slights it," adding that "he marks not whose 'twas first, and aftertimes / May judge it to be his." According to Michell, Shakespeare was most probably the subject of Jonson's epigram.

Fellow dramatist Robert Greene also harbored a grudge, calling Shakespeare "an upstart crow, beautified with our feathers." And well he might, since Michell discloses that *A Winter's Tale* was based on one of Robert Greene's own works, a 1588 prose narrative entitled *Pandosto: The Triumph of Time.*

Neither was Shakespeare picky about which sources he drew upon. Dickson reveals that the Bard plundered "sensationalist romances to serious tomes such as Holinshed's *Chronicles* and Plutarch's *Lives.*" *Hamlet,* Dickson tells us, was an earlier play dubbed the "ur-Hamlet," and *King Lear* was based on *The Chronicle History of King Leir and His Three Daughters.* Arthur Brooke's long narrative poem *The Tragical History of Romeus and Juliet* gave rise to ... you can probably guess that one.

Shakespeare penned just under forty plays, but few have original plots. *Love's Labour's Lost, The Merry Wives of Windsor* (the only play set wholly in Shakespeare's England), and *The Tempest* may be original works, but even *The Tempest* is thought to have been based on a 1609 shipwreck report. It is clear, therefore, that Shakespeare was not an originator of story lines: He was a dramatist. He used established tales to showcase his insightful characterization and sparkling dialogue. It is likely that he probably didn't care who said it first, just who said it best. As twentieth-century poet, critic, and playwright T. S. Eliot confided, "Immature poets imitate; mature poets steal."

Ben Jonson, in a more gracious moment, said of Shakespeare

that "he was not of an age, but for all time!" but not everyone had such positive views on the writer's talent. Irish dramatist George Bernard Shaw, who didn't hold Shakespeare in quite such high regard as he held himself, suggested that the Bard was "for an afternoon, but not for all time."

My own personal views on the matter are that it's much ado about nothing, but all's well that ends well.

VIRGINIA WOOLF WROTE
ALL OF HER BOOKS STANDING UP

LITERARY ICON VIRGINIA WOOLF IS FAMED FOR being an innovative writer and an early feminist. Quentin Bell, Woolf's nephew and biographer, reveals a surprising fact about her writing habits in his celebrated book *Virginia Woolf:* "She had a desk standing about three feet six inches high with a sloping top; it was so high that she had to stand to her work." Virginia was said to have explained this working arrangement in various ways, but Bell claims that "her principal motive was the fact that Vanessa [Virginia's sister and Bell's mother], like many painters, stood to work." Bell explains that Virginia felt her artistic efforts would appear less worthy when compared to those of her sister "unless she set matters on a footing of equality." This is the reason, Bell reveals, that "for many years she stood at this strange desk, and, in a quite unnecessary way, tired herself."

Julia Briggs, writing in *Virginia Woolf: An Inner Life*, confirms this reading of the author's unusual actions, describing Virginia's relationship with her older sister as "passionate and possessive: She adored and imitated her." Briggs explains that when Vanessa began to paint professionally, Virginia took to "writing standing at a high desk, as if working at an easel." Briggs adds that imitating Vanessa proved the existence of "a barely suppressed rivalry."

It is strange to imagine the revered feminist writer striving so hard to appear as impressive as her older sister. The arresting image surely gives us further insight into her unique character. As for the fate of Virginia's three-foot-six-inch writing desk, Professor Hermione Lee informs us in *Virginia Woolf* that it was inherited by Bell and "had its legs chopped down."

Another "Wolf" who stood while writing was novelist Thomas Wolfe. Standing at a height of six foot six, Wolfe eschewed the discomfort of desk-writing, and worked on top of his fridge. Diane Ackerman, writing in *A Natural History of the Senses*, adds that Ernest Hemingway (due to a back injury) and Lewis Carroll also worked in a standing position. Evidently, Ms. Woolf was not alone in employing such an unusual authorial habit.

JAMES BOND AUTHOR IAN FLEMING WROTE THE CHILDREN'S CLASSIC *CHITTY CHITTY BANG BANG*

IAN FLEMING, THE FAMED AUTHOR OF THE DECIDEDLY ADULT JAMES Bond novels, also penned the delightful children's story *Chitty Chitty Bang Bang*, which was first published as three separate tales in 1964 and 1965. *The Cambridge Guide to Children's Books in English* describes how the eponymous car was "restored

from dilapidation by Commander Caractacus Pott." The car, along with the Commander, his wife Mimsie, and their twins then becomes "embroiled with smugglers." The 1968 film version, written by Roald Dahl, follows a different plot, as widower Caractacus Potts, his two children, and a new character called Truly Scrumptious all fall prey to pirates, while Potts's grandfather and children are kidnapped and then rescued by Potts and Truly.

On consideration, perhaps it's not so strange that Fleming should have penned this children's adventure: Both the Bond novels and *Chitty Chitty Bang Bang* feature high adventure and gadget cars. The cars in the Bond films are high-tech, while the counterpart in the children's tale is magical.

Interestingly, it seems that the subject of the story, which was written for Fleming's young son, Caspar, was modeled on a real car. In *The Convertible*, Ken Vose reveals that the *Chitty Chitty Bang Bang* car was based on an actual vehicle built in 1920 by Count Louis Zborowski, the millionaire racing-driver son of a Polish aristocrat. Zborowski designed and built three aeroengined cars known as "Chitty Bang Bang" in Higham Park in Kent. Vose goes on to explain that the original car was "powered by a German Maybach Zeppelin engine" and was famed for winning races speeding along at almost 120 mph. In 1921, a twelve-year-old Fleming is said to have visited the Brooklands motor-racing circuit in Surrey and watched the car race. The Count was tragically killed in the Italian Grand Prix when he crashed into a tree in October 1924. Chitty I (a second model had been built in 1921) was later bought by the sons of Sir Arthur Conan Doyle, and after being temporarily exhibited at Brooklands the car was eventually broken up for parts.

There are further connections between the Bond novels and the magical car. Desmond Llewelyn, famed for his role as Q in the Bond films, also appears in the film version of *Chitty Chitty Bang Bang* as Coggins, the junk dealer who sells Chitty to Caractacus Potts. Gert Fröbe, who plays the villain in *Goldfinger*, features as Baron Bomburst in the children's film.

THE HEART OF NINETEENTH-CENTURY NOVELIST THOMAS HARDY WAS BURIED IN A DIFFERENT LOCATION FROM HIS BODY

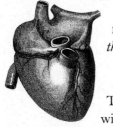

THOMAS HARDY, AUTHOR OF GREAT nineteenth-century novels such as *Far from the Madding Crowd* and *Tess of the D'Urbervilles*, was very fond of his native "Wessex." In *The Life of Thomas Hardy*, English lecturer Paul Turner reveals that "Hardy wanted to rest with his family in...Stinsford Church" in Dorset. Hardy requested to be buried with his first wife, Emma. Theirs had been a strained relationship, and presumably Hardy felt he could make a final, lasting commitment to Emma once he was dead.

According to Turner, however, "the Establishment" had other ideas. "Hardy must have a public burial in Westminster Abbey." After much soul-searching, the result was a rather unsavory compromise of burying the renowned writer in two places. Turner describes how, after Hardy died, his heart was "excised, wrapped in a towel, and kept, as the parlor maid recalled, 'in my biscuit-tin' until the 'heart-burial at Stinsford.'" James Gibson, writing in *Thomas Hardy: A Literary Life*, explains that "the rest of him was cremated and buried in the Abbey."

There is a fanciful adjunct to the story: namely, that before the "heart-burial," Hardy's heart was believed to have been liberated from the biscuit tin by a cat, which had it for tea. The heart was then allegedly replaced with a pig's heart. The story lacks credibility, however, because the facts vary from telling to telling. Sometimes the culprit is

Hardy's cat, other times Hardy's sister's cat, and occasionally the perpetrator is a dog. But the main reason it's unlikely to be true owes much to the testimony of a Dr. Edward Mann, speaking in a 1967 interview with Terry Coleman (coauthor of *Providence & Mr. Hardy*). Dr. Mann explained that although he had overheard the Bishop of Sherborne recounting a version of this very after-dinner story, he knew it to be false because *he* was the doctor who had removed Hardy's heart, and it was *he* who had sealed the tin.

ERNEST V. WRIGHT PENNED A FULL-LENGTH NOVEL WITHOUT USING THE LETTER *E*

ERNEST VINCENT WRIGHT'S 1939 NOVEL *GADSBY: A STORY OF OVER 50,000 Words Without Using the Letter "E"* is about a small town of the title name and the projects it undertakes. In the introduction (which does contain the letter *e*), Wright explains that he ensured this feat was achieved without error by typing "with the *E* type-bar of the typewriter tied down." Wright comments that "people, as a rule, will not stop to realize what a task such an attempt actually is," adding that as he wrote, "a whole army of little *E*s gathered around my desk, all eagerly expecting to be called upon." They weren't.

Here is a short excerpt: "Just why a woman thinks that a grain of dust in a totally inconspicuous spot is such a catastrophic abnormality is hard to say; but if you simply broach a thought that a grain of it might lurk in back of a piano, or up back of an oil painting, a flood of soap-suds will instantly burst forth; and any man who can find any of his things for four days is a clairvoyant, or a magician!" *Gadsby* continues in this *e*-less, if at times convoluted, style. You can read the rest at www.spinelessbooks.com/gadsby.

A similarly lipogrammatic (omitting a specific letter) work is French novelist Georges Perec's 1969 tale, *La Disparition*, which was also written without the letter *e*.

A NONEXISTENT WORD WAS INCLUDED IN WEBSTER'S DICTIONARY

THE "WORD" IN QUESTION WAS "DORD." IN *THE STORY OF WEBSTER'S Third*, Herbert Charles Morton explains that "it was recorded in *Webster's Second* in 1934 on page 771," where it remained undetected for five years. This less than satisfactory position was rectified when, as Morton reveals, "the lack of an etymology for dord…was noted by an editor" and was not "caught and corrected until 1940."

The "ghost word" managed to become included in *Webster's Dictionary* when an editor, who was collating scientific abbrevia-

tions, noted down the scientific abbreviation for density, which can be represented as an uppercase or lowercase *d*, i.e., *D* or *d*. The editor was collecting abbreviations because, unlike in the first edition, it had been decided that they should appear at the back of the dictionary in a separate section rather than be included in the main alphabet. In *Blooming English: Observations on the Roots, Cultivation and Hybrids of the English Language*, Kate Burridge reveals that "somehow this abbreviation got detached and came to be included in the main alphabet," appearing to be a synonym for density. Morton explains that on the note the "or" should have been marked to be set in italics to indicate that the letters were abbreviations. But instead, "D or d" was marked to be set in boldface in the manner of a word entry. Morton quotes Philip Babcock Gove, editor in chief of the third edition, commenting that "as soon as someone else entered the pronunciation...dord was given a slap on the back that sent breath into its being."

Patrick Hanks's contribution to *The Oxford Handbook of Computational Linguistics* confirms that the "ghost word" was "a misreading of the abbreviation 'D *or* d'...which does indeed mean 'density.'"

Burridge reveals that since "dord" made it into *Webster's Dictionary*, it also made it "into others." She also adds that "some (probably the embarrassed editors) have claimed that the ghost word was included to deliberately trap any would-be plagiarists." In the words of Kate Burridge—a likely story!

CHAPTER 2

That's Entertainment

CHARLIE CHAPLIN FAILED TO QUALIFY IN A CHARLIE CHAPLIN LOOK-ALIKE CONTEST

SILENT-SCREEN STAR CHARLIE CHAPLIN MADE HIS NAME IN THE FILM industry of the 1920s, and was famed for his tramp character with the distinctive walk, who made his debut in the 1914 film *Kid Auto Races in Venice*. *The Moviegoer's Companion* (edited by Rhiannon Guy) describes how by 1915 Chaplin's growing fame had begun to spawn Chaplin look-alike competitions, although the aim was to imitate the "Little Tramp" persona rather than Chaplin himself. According to Chaplin biographer Joyce Milton, writing in *Tramp: The Life of Charlie Chaplin*, promising newcomer Bob Hope "took first prize in a Chaplin contest in Cleveland" in 1915. In his autobiography *Bob Hope: My Life in Jokes*, Hope reveals how he used to parade about in Chaplin-style makeup in his youth, and was once rewarded for his efforts: "I was persuaded into entering a [look-alike] contest at Luna Park.... The result was the number-one prize—a new cooking stove for Mom."

Comedian Lou Costello also had a similar start to his career in the early 1920s, when he too won "a Charlie Chaplin look-alike contest," according to Meredith Arms Bzdak and Douglas Petersen, writing in *Public Sculpture in New Jersey.*

Personality Comedians as Genre author Wes D. Gehring says that Chaplin entered one such contest "as a lark," but Milton confirms that in the San Francisco theater where it was held, Chaplin "failed to even make the finals." How upsetting!

Despite his lack of success in the competition, Milton records that Chaplin took the defeat in good heart, commenting to a reporter, "I am tempted to give lessons in the Chaplin walk...out of pity as well as in the desire to see the thing done correctly."

ELVIS PRESLEY CONSISTENTLY FAILED TO WIN TALENT CONTESTS

ROCK 'N' ROLL LEGEND ELVIS PRESLEY, ALSO KNOWN as "The King," appears to have been less than legendary when entering talent contests. It's often claimed, says Todd Slaughter in *The Elvis Archives,* that at the tender age of ten, Elvis entered a talent contest at the Mississippi-Alabama Fair and Dairy Show in 1945, and came away with second prize. "It wasn't so," Slaughter corrects. "Elvis...was placed fifth, which entitled him to free rides on the fairground attractions." Doubtless this was an excellent reward for an impecunious ten-year-old.

Curtis W. Ellison, in *Country Music Culture,* confirms that Elvis did indeed manage to win fifth place in the 1945 contest, and goes on to reveal that ten years later, Elvis auditioned for the radio show *Grand Ole Opry* and "placed second" behind a Linda Coker of Gulfport, Mississippi.

Even when famous, Elvis still failed to snatch that elusive first prize. Interviewed in the 1996 documentary *The Burger and the*

King, steakhouse owner Lil Thomson tells of the time she and her husband held a talent contest: "My husband could talk you into anything. He said, 'Elvis, would you get up and sing for us?' Nobody even said a word—[they] gave a few applause—that was about it. He came in third place."

This merely confirms what we all know to be the case: True talent will shine, regardless of the pronouncements of those who judge.

HOLLYWOOD HEARTTHROB CLARK GABLE WAS ENTERED IN THE LOCAL BIRTH REGISTER AS FEMALE

THE CLAIM THAT CLARK GABLE WAS REGISTERED AS A GIRL AT BIRTH is a commonly repeated piece of Hollywood trivia. It appears in many of his unofficial online biographies. The assertion is strange, but true, and the explanatory story is even stranger.

In 1901, in Cadiz, Ohio, the arrival of a baby boy prompted the child's itinerant oil field-worker father William Gable to register the birth in the name of Clark Gable. (According to biographer Chrystopher J. Spicer, writing in *Clark Gable*, it was only in later life that Gable "turned Clark into his middle name by adding William in front of it.")

On page 107 of the Cadiz Record of Births (reproduced in Spicer's book), opposite the entry for Gable, "the county records clerk...wrote both *M* and *F* in the gender columns, and then later crossed them out and reentered *M*." To the casual observer, it looks as though there was some confusion over Gable's gender, yet William Gable described his ten-and-a-half-pound newborn as "a real he-man from the start."

The confusion was not due to Gable's gender, however, but to the delivery physician, Dr. Campbell, who "had typically illegible doctor's handwriting." This meant that the clerk was unable to read the doctor's notes on the baby's sex. Relying upon the father to provide such technical information was, seemingly, out of the question, so the registrar devised a novel way around the problem. Spicer reveals that he "wrote in both [genders] to be on the safe side until it could be checked with Dr. Campbell personally." One solution, perhaps, but not a particularly fair one for baby Clark or his proud father, who pointed out that Gable junior was built like a "regular blacksmith."

BAD BOY OF ROCK OZZY OSBOURNE
BIT THE HEAD OFF A LIVE BAT

(STOP READING NOW IF YOU ARE SQUEAMISH.) THE LOCATION IS Des Moines, Iowa. The date is January 1982. John "Ozzy" Osbourne, front man for Black Sabbath, is live in concert, and an unsuspecting bat is duly hurled onto the stage by an overzealous fan.

In *Diary of a Madman: Ozzy Osbourne*, biographer Carol Clerk records the singer's reactions. "I thought it was a plastic toy....So I just grabbed this thing, bit the head off and thought, 'Goodness gracious [or words to that effect]! It was flapping.'"

Throughout the tour, Ozzy and his band had gotten used to dodging rubber snakes and plastic rats as they were thrown onstage during the gigs, and so he had quite naturally assumed that the bat was just another inanimate object for him to have some fun with. Recalling the incident later, Osbourne remarked that he hadn't particularly enjoyed the flavor of the bat, which he described as "all crunchy and warm." He added, "It's still stuck in my...throat, after all these years." Not literally, we hope (although that would explain a lot).

Clerk quotes Osbourne bemoaning the fact that people keep

asking if he still does it. He is quick to undeceive them: "It happened...once, for Christ's sake." Journalist John Walsh's article, included in *Into the Void* (edited by Barney Hoskyns), confirms that Ozzy's bat has become something of an albatross. Walsh quotes Osbourne stating that he believes "And he bit the head off a bat" may well be his epitaph.

Even more unpleasant than the taste of bat, Clerk reveals, "was the course of painful antirabies injections that the singer then had to undergo" after the unfortunate event. According to biographer Sue Crawford in *Ozzy*, the Black Sabbath front man dealt with the trauma by "barking like a dog" as he waited for the first injection, and making jokes about the likely effects of having rabies. In reality, however, the situation was far from amusing, and Ozzy suffered badly while receiving the weeklong course of injections, and even collapsed a number of times during the rest of the tour.

It's difficult to decide who had it worse: Ozzy or the ill-fated bat....

IN THE FILM *THE WIZARD OF OZ*, THE ORIGINAL TIN MAN, BUDDY EBSEN, WAS NEARLY KILLED BY HIS MAKEUP

WHEN MGM'S PRESTIGIOUS 1939 MUSICAL *THE WIZARD OF OZ* WAS being cast, Broadway star Ray Bolger landed the part of the Tin Man. Also contracted to MGM was up-and-coming actor Buddy Ebsen, who was cast as the Scarecrow. In *Flights of Fancy*, Kenneth Von Gunden explains that Ebsen, with his tall frame, looked every inch the Scarecrow, but because Bolger had set his heart on that particular part, good-natured Ebsen "readily agreed to switch parts with Bolger."

This act of generosity was to be Ebsen's undoing. Von Gunden reveals that ten days into filming, Ebsen, having gone home to relax after a hard day on the set, "took a breath and nothing happened." MGM producer Mervyn LeRoy's contribution to *The Grove Book of Hollywood* adds that Ebsen's wife "rushed him to the hospital where they had to put him in an iron lung." According to LeRoy, the reason for Ebsen's bout of ill-health was because "Jack Dawn...head makeup man...[had] sprayed him with aluminum dust."

Dawn's innovative but deadly makeup nearly cost Ebsen his life. He spent two weeks in Los Angeles's Good Samaritan Hospital due to what Von Gunden describes as "an allergic reaction to the aluminum powder" contained in his makeup. In *The Wizardry of Oz*, Jay Scarfone and William Stillman state that Ebsen suffered this "near-fatal" reaction "because he inhaled powder with each application" which, in the words of Ebsen, "coated my lungs with paint." In *Costumes and Chemistry*, Sylvia Moss confirms that "working with powders can damage lungs, eyes, and skin" for the simple reason that "metal powders are absorbed into the skin or respiratory system and can damage blood, kidneys, lungs, and brain." LeRoy laments that "Ebsen had been the guinea pig and had lost a great part because of it."

Having lost their Tin Man, Von Gunden explains that MGM "borrowed Jack Haley from 20th Century-Fox to take over the role." LeRoy says that this time Dawn "didn't use aluminum dust, but made a paste of the aluminum and spread that on Haley's face" and all was well, at least for Haley.

In *The Making of The Wizard of Oz*, Aljean Harmetz comments that after this unfortunate turn, Ebsen's career "whether coincidentally or not—went into a slump." Harmetz adds that Ebsen "did not resurface with any permanence until 1956, when he appeared as the sidekick to Fess Parker in Disney's *Davy Crockett*." However, Ebsen did manage to carve himself a new career in time and went on to play Jed Clampett in the long-running TV sitcom *The Beverly Hillbillies* and later the title role in the television detective series *Barnaby Jones*, which ran for seven years. He also appeared in *The Andersonville Trial* and *Breakfast at Tiffany's*.

CHAPTER 3

The Animal World

A CROCODILE'S JAWS CAN BE HELD SHUT BY A HUMAN HAND

A CROCODILE CAN SNAP ITS JAWS SHUT WITH A FORCE OF UP TO 3,000 pounds per square inch compared to just 100 pounds for a large dog. In *The Illustrated Encyclopedia of Animals,* Fran Pickering puts these statistics into perspective by revealing that a crocodile's bite is so strong that it can "crush the bones of a small animal." Having said that, in *Crocodiles & Alligators* wildlife author Seymour Simon informs us that "the muscles that open the jaws are weaker," adding that some people can hold the jaws of a crocodile shut "with their hands." Pickering goes further, suggesting that their jaws can be held shut with just "one hand." (Not one to try at home, children.)

This revelation would explain the South Florida practice of alligator wrestling. Peggy A. Bulger's book *South Florida Folklife* divulges some of its secrets: "Keep the 'gator well fed, grab it by the snout so it can't open its jaws, flip it on its back and stroke it to sleep—then pretend to be struggling valiantly with the beast for a long time so as to earn big tips."

I was about to speak out against this dubious "sport," but since discovering that the alligator gets a good lunch followed by a nice nap, it doesn't quite seem like such a bad deal.

MALE SEAHORSES GIVE BIRTH TO THEIR YOUNG

THE GRACEFUL LITTLE SEAHORSE'S CLAIM TO FAME IS, AS NEIL Garrick-Maidment reveals in *Practical Fishkeeping: Seahorses*, "the male's ability to get pregnant." As the *Encyclopaedia Britannica* explains, "the male, not the female, carries the fertilized eggs."

Herpetologist and conservation biologist Frank Indiviglio, writing in *Seahorses*, describes how "courtship can be lengthy—up to ten hours in certain species. It involves spiraling…and swimming about with tails interlocked." He adds that "the female produces the eggs, but the male carries them in a special pouch on the underside of the tail."

Garrick-Maidment claims that unlike other baby-carrying males, "the seahorse has a true pregnancy, feeding its young through a placenta," while Indiviglio explains that the embryos embed in the pouch's epithelial tissue, and oxygen is supplied by capillaries. In *Dwarf Seahorses*, Ailsa Wagner-Abbott confides that "dwarf males have been reported to collect eggs from a number of different females in succession, to form a single brood." According to *Britannica*, "the eggs, deposited in a brood pouch beneath the male's tail by the female, remain there until they hatch."

You might think that, after having suffered one pregnancy, the male seahorse would be reluctant to undergo the process again, but according to Garrick-Maidment, although exhausted "he will usually get pregnant again within forty-eight hours." What selfless heroes of the sea world!

CHOCOLATE IS POISONOUS TO DOGS

THE WHIMSICAL CONCEPT OF DEATH BY CHOCOLATE is only too real for a dog that wolfs down a 100-gram chocolate bar, according to the *Handbook of Poisoning in Dogs and Cats.* Dogs love chocolate, but it doesn't love them! Chocolate contains theobromine, a compound with similar properties to caffeine. David Ropeik and George Gray, authors of *Risk: A Practical Guide for Deciding What's Really Safe and What's Really Dangerous in the World Around You*, state that theobromine "is unique in its toxicity for dogs."

According to animal-science specialist Linda P. Case of the University of Illinois, writing in *The Dog: Its Behavior, Nutrition and Health*, "theobromine is toxic to dogs when consumed in large quantities." The authors of the *Handbook of Poisoning in Dogs and Cats*, Alexander Campbell and Michael Chapman, back this up: "Theobromine directly stimulates both the myocardium and the CNS [central nervous system]." Case explains that theobromine can be deadly to dogs because it passes through their bodies very slowly. For example, it would take an adult dog around seventeen hours to rid itself of the chemical, whereas in a human it would only take a third of the time. Case adds that "as little as three ounces of baking chocolate could be fatal to a twenty-five-pound dog."

Yet, chocolate is sold specifically

for dogs. The important point here is that it isn't real chocolate: only a chocolate-*flavored* treat. My husband, Andy, can testify to this, because as a child he once made the mistake of sampling his dog's chocolate. His verdict? The dog was welcome to it.

Can chocolate, eaten to excess, be harmful to humans? The good news is that it can only be a health risk if an inordinate amount is consumed. *Food Poisoning*, written by professor of biochemistry Anthony T. Tu, reassures us that "a consumption greater than 7.5 to 10 pounds of milk chocolate per day" would be required. What? Is that considered excessive?

LIZARDS ARE SOLAR-POWERED AND CAN GROW NEW TAILS

LIZARDS ARE ECTOTHERMIC, WHICH IS OFTEN DESCRIBED AS "COLD-blooded," but as James H. Harding explains in *Amphibians and Reptiles of the Great Lakes Region*, this does not make reptiles cold to the touch as is commonly supposed. It simply means that they are dependent on the temperature of their surroundings for heat. In Eric R. Pianka and Laurie J. Vitt's informative work *Lizards*, they explain that "the ultimate source of heat for lizards is the sun." Such animals are called heliotherms, from the Greek word for sun, *hēlios*.

Brian K. McNab, author of *The Physiological Ecology of Vertebrates*, agrees: "The maintenance of a temperature differential by a heliotherm requires exposure to the sun." Pianka and Vitt add that "many lizards take advantage of sunlight by seeking out patches of direct sunlight exposure in their habitats and basking to gain heat." In the mornings, lizards must bask in direct sunlight to absorb sufficient heat to allow them to dart about. A cold lizard will have great difficulty escaping a predator.

The lizard's most spectacular defense mechanism is, as Pianka and Vitt point out, its "tail autotomy," which is more commonly known as "tail loss." Many lizards have specially adapted "weak fracture planes" within certain tail vertebrae, and tail stubs heal easily and quickly. Pianka and Vitt claim that the loss of its tail has surprisingly little effect on a lizard's behavior, as individuals will "often resume basking" after becoming separated from their tails, seemingly unfazed by the experience.

However, other lizard species with "tough tails" usually cannot regenerate a very complete tail if their original should happen to be lost. In the wild, a high percentage of lizards have a regenerated tail, indicating that many a lizard has escaped at least once by this method.

ELECTRIC EELS DO PRODUCE ELECTRICITY

THE CYNICS AMONG US COULD BE FORGIVEN FOR IMAGINING THAT these elongated South American fish got their name because, as they swim along, they perhaps generate a bit of static electricity. But according to Alvin and Virginia Silverstein, writing in *Nature's Champions*, this sea creature is "a living stor-  age battery." (They aren't true eels...but that's another story.)

A Neotropical Companion author John Kricher warns that they can "emit a jolt of 650 volts," which is more than five times the voltage used to power electrical items in a standard American home. For this reason, Kricher advises that they are to be "appreciated from a respectable distance."

As well as for protection, eels use this electricity to find their way around, much like sharks and bats. They may also use the electric current to communicate with other eels. As the

Silversteins explain, electric eels produce the current by compacting their organs into the front fifth of their body and packing the remaining space with "more than five thousand tiny electric generators." Author of *The Facts About Electricity* Rebecca Hunter adds that horses standing in shallow water have been "knocked over by the electricity produced by electric eels," while *Travellers' Health* (edited by Richard M. Dawood) features a warning that electric eels are "capable of killing an adult human."

Eels haven't always been regarded as detrimental to humans, however, for *Technological Trajectories and the Human Environment* (edited by Jesse H. Ausubel and H. Dale Langford) reveals that in the eighteenth century "scientists reported that electric eels cured gout." No doubt several gout-ridden gentry found out the hard way that they didn't.

In the early twentieth century, Robert W. Rydell describes a "compelling scientific demonstration" in his book *World of Fairs*. A current generated by an electric eel, which was wired up in a New York Zoological Society exhibit, provided enough power to "ignite magnesium flares along the Great White Way" (Broadway); undoubtedly a more spectacular use of them than for boring old medicinal purposes.

RABBITS' TEETH NEVER STOP GROWING

IN THE WILD, A RABBIT'S SURVIVAL IS DEPENDENT ON ITS ABILITY TO chew and chew...and chew, which naturally creates a great deal of wear on its teeth. Writing in *Zooarchaeology*, Elizabeth J. Reitz and Elizabeth S. Wing explain that "many mammalian teeth have roots that close when the tooth is fully erupted." However, in the case of rabbits, "adult teeth with open roots continue to grow throughout the life of the animal," so that its "capacity to chew with a tooth which still has a strong enamel surface is not diminished."

Karen Gendron, author of *The Rabbit Handbook*, points out that rabbits' teeth grow "at a rate of 3.9 to 4.7 inches a year," and adds that "if the teeth are not worn down and do not press against each other, they will overgrow, leading to quite bizarre twists and turns of the teeth as they grow."

In *Rabbitlopaedia*, Meg Brown and Virginia Richardson confirm that a rabbit's teeth "grow constantly throughout its lifetime." They explain that rabbits rely on an even chewing motion to grind their teeth down. If teeth become out of line, however, "they over-grow," which can result in a painful condition for pet bunnies.

In *All About Your Rabbit*, Bradley Viner advises avoiding this situation by ensuring that a pet rabbit is fed "a high-fiber diet with plenty of hay, grass and green food," which will "encourage normal chewing, and promote better tooth health."

Incidentally, *The Oxford Library of Words and Phrases* reveals that the word "bunny" comes from the seventeenth-century Scottish Gaelic word *bun*, meaning "squirrel." I wonder what seventeenth-century Gaelic speakers used to call squirrels, then?

THE SEX OF REPTILES IS DETERMINED BY HEAT

THE SEX OF HUMAN BABIES IS DECIDED AT CONCEPTION BY CHROMO-somes, but this is not so for many baby reptiles. Authors Kenneth M. Weiss and Anne V. Buchanan, writing in *Genetics and the Logic of Evolution*, reveal that for reptiles "factors in the environment" do the job instead of genetics. In turtles, for example, "sex determination is temperature-dependent."

Don and Edward O. Moll, authors of *The Ecology, Exploitation and Conservation of River Turtles*, clarify this by explaining that "the temperature at which the eggs are incubated determines the sex of the hatchlings in many species." Zug, Vitt, and Caldwell, authors of *Herpetology: An Introductory Biology of Amphibians and Reptiles,* agree: "Sex determination usually occurs in the second trimester of development." They add that the average temperature in the nest during that period decides the sex of the baby reptiles. In general, high temperatures produce females and low temperatures produce males.

According to the Molls, temperature-dependent sex determination in reptiles was first reported in M. Charnier's 1966 research paper on the agama lizard—"Action of Temperature on the Sex Ratio in the *Agama agama* (*Agamidae, Lacertilia*) Embryo." They also comment that "incubating eggs in containers or in buildings can . . . alter the natural sex ratios of hatchlings." This information has a practical application since, as Zug, Vitt, and Caldwell explain, "as soon as it was learned that sea turtles had temperature-dependent sex determination . . . artificial incubation was abandoned." These days, if sea turtles are artificially incubated, their temperature is carefully gauged to match what would have been their natural nest environment.

GIRAFFES HAVE THE SAME NUMBER OF VERTEBRAE AS HUMANS

THE STATELY GIRAFFE HAS A NECK THAT MEASURES FIVE TO SIX FEET in length. According to Walter W. Skeat's *The Concise Dictionary of English Etymology,* the word "giraffe" is thought to come via the Arabic *zaráf* from the Egyptian *soraphé,* which means (not surprisingly) "long neck." Yet it is a surprising fact that, as noted by Barbara Keevil Parker in *Giraffes,* the mammals have just seven vertebrae, although each vertebra is ten inches long. More interesting still, William Howells's book *Getting Here: The Story of Human Evolution* reveals that (with just a couple of exceptions) every mammal "has exactly seven vertebrae in its neck, from giraffe to dolphin."

Nineteenth-century German biologist Ernst Haeckel explains the reason in *The Evolution of Man*: "This constant number...is strong proof of the common descent of the mammals: It can only be explained by faithful heredity from a common stem-form, a primitive mammal with seven cervical vertebrae." In *Primate Anatomy*, modern-day anthropologist Dr. Friderun Ankel-Simons agrees that in the neck region there are "seven vertebrae in almost all mammals." (The exceptions are the two-toed tree sloth with six, and the three-toed tree sloth with up to ten.)

As a point of interest, giraffes are seldom heard and are popularly thought to have no vocal cords, and are also supposed to be mute. However, giraffes are perfectly capable of making sounds, which the *Encyclopaedia Britannica* describes as "low calls and moans."

CHAPTER 4

Birds *and* Insects

IN MEDIEVAL TIMES, BLACKBIRDS WERE BAKED IN PIES

TO THE MODERN EAR, MANY OLD NURSERY RHYMES SOUND LIKE MYS-
terious coded messages, only intelligible to those in the know.
The following sixteenth-century rhyme is no exception: "Sing a
song of sixpence, / A pocket full of rye; / Four and twenty blackbirds, / Baked in a pie. / When the pie was opened, / The birds
began to sing; / Was not that a dainty
dish, / To set before the King?" This
particular verse, the subject of a recent Internet hoax which claimed the
origins of the rhyme came from a coded
message used to recruit crew members to pirate ships, has, in fact,
no connection with pirates or secret codes whatsoever.

The Oxford Dictionary of Nursery Rhymes (edited by Iona and
Peter Opie) informs us that the most probable explanation is the
most straightforward: It's a description of a form of "entertain-
ment," namely pies containing live wildlife.

Alan Davidson, author of *The Oxford Companion to Food*,
agrees, and suggests that the "allusion must be to the medieval

conceits known as subtleties, which often featured such surprises." The *Companion* quotes an Italian cookery book of 1549 that included a recipe "to make pies so that birds may be alive in them and flie [*sic*] out when it is cut up." Writing in *Recipes for Disaster: A Deliciously Funny Feast of Culinary Catastrophes*, Richard De'Ath describes a similar 1625 recipe: "The pie of coarse pastry is baked first, then allowed to cool, after which, birds (sometimes frogs) are pushed in through holes in the bottom of the crust." The author of this seventeenth-century recipe then assures us that "their fluttering (or jumping) to freedom when the pie is cut open causes much delight and pleasure to the whole company." Of course that all depends on whether you enjoy live animals bursting forth from your lunch!

However, that's not to say that blackbirds weren't also used as pie filling. De'Ath reveals that in the sixteenth century wild birds were often caught for food. *The Oxford Companion to Food* informs us that they were incorporated into pies in the Middle Ages: "Dumplings stuffed with sparrows or larks graced many a table." De'Ath adds that the Welsh were particularly fond of "Pickled Puffin."

Linda J. Dickinson, writing in *A Price Guide to Cookbooks and Recipe Leaflets*, cites an 1891 recipe advising "four and twenty blackbirds" would require "a medium-size baking dish." So how big were the "large-size" baking dishes? In *Secrets of the Great Old-Timey Cooks*, Barbara Swell refers to a 1933 recipe for "blackbird pie" from the *Home Comfort Cookbook* that advises preparing the blackbirds in the same manner as pigeons. Finally, De'Ath confirms that "blackbirds are still, to this day, used in pies or to make terrines" in a few regions of Europe.

MALE EMUS INCUBATE AND REAR THEIR CHICKS

IN LARGE FLIGHTLESS BIRDS, SUCH AS THE Australian emu, the African ostrich, and the South American rhea, the sex roles are reversed. Gisela Kaplan and Lesley J. Rogers explain in *Birds: Their Habits and Skills* that "the emu male incubates the eggs, usually of several females, and then guards his chicks until they are seven months old." In *The Encyclopedia of Birds* (edited by ornithology professor Christopher Perrins), the Australian cassowary (a smaller relative of the emu) is also described as taking on the traditional female role: "The male incubates the four to eight eggs in a nest on the forest floor." Not only does he incubate the chicks, but he also selflessly accompanies them "for about a year before returning to his solitary life."

Zoology lecturer T. H. Clutton-Brock explains in *The Evolution of Parental Care* that this method of chick rearing is apparently confined to species where "more than one female lays in the same nest." Such a system of breeding may have evolved from females simply dumping eggs in handy nests or possibly laying eggs in the nests of female relatives. From the male's point of view, collecting a large clutch of eggs from different females means that he is able to further his genes more effectively by raising a larger number of chicks, and therefore making it well worth the extra effort that he invests in caring for them.

In *Biology, Medicine and Surgery of South American Wild Animals* (edited by Murray E. Fowler), we learn that with rheas— large flightless birds related to the ostrich—egg incubation and chick rearing are "carried out exclusively by males." The same volume confirms that, in the case of the tinamou, a South

American bird, "the males incubate the eggs and rear the chicks." The New Zealand kiwi chick incubation is also carried out "by the male."

The phenomenon is also found in other species of birds. In *Shorebirds*, Arthur Morris reveals that female sandpipers "arrive first on the breeding grounds and select and defend territories." Morris adds that "it is the females who aggressively court the males" but it is the males who "incubate the eggs and tend the young." Thus, it would appear that in some areas of the bird community, males can make excellent mothers.

PARROTS CAN LIVE FOR UP TO ONE HUNDRED YEARS

MANY BIRDS, PARTICULARLY SMALL GARDEN BIRDS, HAVE SHORT LIFE spans, and live only for a couple of seasons. Conversely, large birds can survive for many decades, in some cases outliving their human owners. Parrot-care manuals advise their readers to think carefully about buying a parrot, because such a purchase could turn into a lifelong commitment. As indicated in *The Second-Hand Parrot* by Mattie Sue Athan and Dianalee Deter, some parrots and cockatoos can live longer than their owners, and "some birds may need more time to acclimatize than others."

Small Animal Care and Management author Dean M. Warren states that macaws "are hardy, long-lived birds that may live for seventy-five years or more." In *Parrots* Sima Rabinowitz goes further, revealing that "macaws often live for more than a hundred years." The *Encyclopaedia Britannica* states that "claims of eighty or even a hundred years are frequent" for parrots. The oldest parrot-type bird on official record was a male sulphur-crested cockatoo called Cocky who lived in the London Zoo and died in 1982, aged at least eighty.

As a point of interest, Winston Churchill's fabled 104-year-old macaw, Charlie, who was said to refer to Hitler in "unfavorable terms," turned out to be just that, a fable. Lady Soames, DBE, Churchill's youngest daughter, set the record straight in a letter to *Finest Hour* (Winter 2002–3, No. 117), the *Journal of the Churchill Centre and Societies.* Lady Soames stated: "My father never owned a Macaw in the Thirties or at any other time as far as I am aware." She went on to explain that he did own "an African Grey Parrot in the mid to late Thirties." She described the parrot as "quite disagreeable," explaining that it frequently bit those "who tried to curry favor with it." She added that "the bird did not spend the war at my father's side," and expressed the hope that the publication would "correct this tiresome, though trivial, inaccuracy."

FLAMINGOS ARE PINK BECAUSE OF THEIR DIET

ONE OF THE MORE GLAMOROUS OF THE BIRD SPECIES IS THE PINK flamingo. These waders are a fetching shade of rose, deepening in places to a deep salmon pink. Yet Kerry K. Karukstis and Gerald R. Van Hecke, writing in their informative work *Chemistry Connections*, explain that young flamingos have "white coloring." They only turn pink if they eat a specific diet that includes "carotenoid-containing small crustaceans, insects and red algae." *Carotenoids as Colourants and Vitamin A Precursors* (edited by J. Christopher Bauernfeind) adds that "pink flamingos on a low-carotenoid diet lose their characteristic feather color."

Professor Klaus Urich, author of *Comparative Animal Biochemistry*, agrees that the flamingo's pink color "stems from the ingestion of astaxanthin and can-thaxanthin from their shrimp diet." Michael Rutter in *Genes and Behavior* explains: "Their color is entirely dependent on the environmental influence of diet." He adds that the flamingo's ability to turn pink is genetically inbuilt: "You could feed seagulls forever on the same diet and they would never turn pink."

(A specific diet is just one way to pigment feathers. Karukstis and Van Hecke also point out that color can arise from pigments in the feather itself, such as the red color of the cardinal bird. Other coloring arises from variations in the feather structure: Microscopic structures on the feather surface of the blue jay "act as tiny prisms to reflect light to create the blue appearance.")

It's also true that flamingos, who sleep in water, do so while standing on one leg. This is to prevent their body heat from escaping into the water. In *1001 Questions Answered About Birds, Insects and the Seashore*, Allan and Helen Cruickshank explain that the birds achieve this by holding their body in an "oblique position," using strong muscles balancing between their knees, which are high up just below their feathers. The lower visible joint is actually their ankle, and that is why it bends backward.

Flamingos were named for their coloring, but the word doesn't derive from "flaming." Adrian Room, editor of *Cassell's Dictionary of Word Histories*, reveals that the Spanish-derived "flamingo," meaning "ruddy," dates back to a sixteenth-century perception of the "ruddy complexion of the Flemish or Dutch."

My grandmother used to refer to Spanish flamenco dancing as "Spanish flamingo dancing," which, as a child, I found hilarious, but as it turns out she wasn't so far off the mark—flamingo and flamenco (via the Spanish word *flamengo*) share the same root, being associated with the Latin *flamma*, meaning "flame": The dancers were thought to take on the same ruddy complexion as that attributed to the Flemish.

EARWIGS ARE SO CALLED BECAUSE THEY CRAWL INTO PEOPLE'S EARS

I WAS GOING TO INCLUDE THIS STATEMENT AS A ludicrous fallacy in *The Pedant's Revolt* until my friend Paula Evans set me straight on the matter. Having spent the night in an RV, Paula awoke with an unsettling sensation in her left ear "like the feeling of trapped water." Eventually, after a series of judicious bangs to her right temple, Paula succeeded in dislodging from her ear a live earwig. According to Paula, it didn't remain alive for very long after.

The Oxford English Dictionary reveals that the word "earwig," that is, "ear wiggler," dates back to the first century A.D., and that the insect was "so called from the notion that it penetrates into the head through the ear." The charge seems to be leveled in many languages. In Latin, the creature is termed *Forficula auricularia* or "scissor ear," as it is in French *perce-oreille* (ear-piercer), Spanish *tijereta*, and Italian *forbicina*. The German *Ohrwurm*, "ear-worm," implies a similar finding (but not so snippy).

First-century Roman natural historian Pliny even passes on a home remedy for dealing with the condition: "If an earwig...be gotten into the eare...spit into the same, and it will come forth anon." A friend must have been required to oblige, since I doubt it's possible to spit into one's own ear. In "A Tale of a Trumpet," poet Thomas Hood demonstrated that the belief was still going strong in the nineteenth century, with his comic line, "No verbal message was worth a pin / Though you hired an earwig to carry it in!"

However, these victimized insects were so named long before it was discovered whether they were invading people's ears on purpose. People's ear canals are clearly not the insect's natural habitat, but they are sometimes mistaken for such. This is because earwigs favor small, round crevices in which to hide; a fact to which any flower arranger who has injudiciously shaken a dahlia will testify. Ear invasions by earwigs are rare, even more so nowadays since we no longer sleep on straw mattresses.

One last but vital point remains to be clarified: Earwigs may wander into your ear by accident, but there is no truth in the assertion implied in the Latin and French names that they bore into the head and lay eggs in the brain. That *would* be abusing your hospitality.

Nowadays, if Paula sleeps in an RV, she does so with cotton balls firmly secured in both ears. I think I might do the same....

ONLY MALE CANARIES SING (WELL)

IF YOU BOUGHT YOUR CANARY FOR A song, don't be surprised if you get what you pay for! Female canaries can often be bought far more cheaply than males. The simple reason is that, generally speaking, females don't sing. Nineteenth-century naturalist Charles Darwin noted in his work *Descent of Man and Selection in Relation to Sex* that, in the case of birds, "the males of most species sing so much better and more continuously than the females." However, in those days the reason was not well defined.

In *Hormones, Sex, and Society: Science of Physicology*, Helmuth Nyborg states the interesting fact that "male canaries sing...

while female birds and castrated males mostly keep quiet." Silverstein, Silverstein, and Silverstein Nunn, writing in *Beautiful Birds*, confirm that "some females sing, but their song is not as pleasant or as varied as the male's." Author of *Indoor Zoo* Michael Elsohn Ross adds that "the older the male canary, the more different songs he sings." The Silversteins advise that "if you want a singing canary, you should get a male."

The phenomenon, of course, has a rational explanation. Nyborg claims that "male singing elicits in the hormonally prepared female canary a cascade of endocrine [hormonal] reactions." *Animal Behavior* author Mark Ridley explains more succinctly: "Males sing in order to attract females."

The same holds true for parakeets, budgerigars, and cockatiels. Many people purchase a budgerigar in the hope that it will make a chatty little companion. In *The Complete Home Veterinary Guide* author Chris C. Pinney explains that male parakeets "have the ability to learn a broad vocabulary," whereas females "won't talk as much as will the opposite sex!" In the world of birds it would appear that, yet again, the gender roles are reversed.

CHAPTER 5

Facts *on* Food

BRAZIL NUTS CONTAIN RADIOACTIVITY

PEOPLE STARE AT ME AGHAST WHEN I MENTION THAT BRAZIL NUTS are radioactive, but it's not as scary as it sounds. The *Encyclopaedia Britannica* explains that "radioactive decay is a property of several naturally occurring elements." In fact, naturally occurring radiation is present all around us; for example, some foodstuffs contain minute traces of radioactivity in the form of the element radium. In *Naturally Occurring Radioactive Material*, Philip T. Underhill comments that "a food containing unusually high quantities of radium is the Brazil nut." R. C. Turner and colleagues first presented this finding in their 1958 research paper "The Naturally Occurring Alpha-ray Activity of Foods." The trees absorb the radium via their extensive root systems and not from the surrounding soil as many believe.

A 2005 study by S. J. Watson and colleagues states that "Brazil nuts can contain elevated levels of radium isotopes," giving a dose of about "0.1 mSv [microsievert] per Brazil nut" compared to a computed tomography (CT) chest X ray, which would give a dose of 8,000 mSv. However, this does not mean that Brazil nuts are dangerous to eat. The radioactivity contained within each nut really is a tiny amount. A 1969 study by J. J. Gabay and N. I. Sax—"Retention of Radium Due to Ingestion of Brazil Nuts," published in *Health Physics*—found that most of the radium from the consumption of Brazil nuts is not retained in the body.

Other foods that contain traces of radioactivity include mussels and bananas.

RED KIDNEY BEANS CAN BE FATAL
IF EATEN UNDERCOOKED

ARE NUTRITIONISTS BEING PARANOID HERE? CAN THE HUMBLE RED kidney bean really be responsible for illness and fatalities? Yes. In the 1970s there was a spate of student illnesses related to consuming chili con carne made in slow cookers. In *Is It Safe to Eat?* Dr. Ian Shaw warns that "red kidney beans contain a group of toxins called lectins." One particular lectin, phasin, is highly toxic and causes blood clots. Shaw points out that "this rapidly results in severe harm or death, because the clots block important small blood vessels (e.g., the brain's blood supply), and diminish the function of 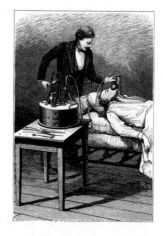 crucial organs." Dean O. Cliver and Hans P. Riemann, writing in *Foodborne Diseases*, confirm that "lectins from kidney beans cause nausea, abdominal pain, vomiting, and bloody diarrhea." Not quite as terminal as Dr. Shaw's findings, but equally to be avoided. They do add, however, that "it only takes five micrograms per kilogram of body weight to kill a human," explaining that this amount "could be present in only one or two beans."

But it's not all bad news where red kidney beans are concerned. Cliver and Riemann explain that, fortunately, the toxin is "deactivated by heat." Therefore, soaking overnight, washing, and boiling "significantly reduces the level of toxic protein and so makes the beans safer." The students became ill because their slow cookers did not reach a high enough temperature to deactivate the toxin. If in doubt, Shaw advises using canned beans, since the canning process subjects the beans to a temperature of 250°F(121°C). Broad beans also contain a small amount of the same toxin, and they should not be eaten raw either. As for why plants contain toxins, Shaw suggests that the compounds have "insecticide properties."

In the past, primitive societies have made use of the toxins in beans to establish guilt or innocence in trials. In *Pills, Potions and Poisons*, professor of pharmacology Trevor Stone and Dr. Gail Darlington describe how the calabar bean was used in northwest Africa up until the mid-1800s. The accused was required to eat the calabar beans, then march before the king until symptoms appeared. These symptoms included intense thirst, profuse salivation, and secretions in the intestine and lungs. Death usually followed in about half an hour. This might appear to be a somewhat rough type of justice, but the guilty tended to nibble the beans slowly, giving time for the toxins to take full effect, whereas the innocent gobbled them down with confidence, promptly vomited them up, and survived the ordeal. So the system worked— kind of.

APPLE SEEDS CONTAIN CYANIDE

MOTHERS ARE OFTEN HEARD TELLING THEIR OFFSPRING NOT TO EAT apple seeds. It's generally followed with the admonishment that an apple tree will grow inside their tummies. Although I think it's fair to say that the accuracy of this statement is to be doubted, it's also true that there may be a good reason to discourage children from eating apple seeds because, as professor of biochemical toxicology John A. Timbrell writes in *Introduction to Toxicology*, "naturally occurring cyanides...are found in the pits and seeds of fruits such as apricots, peaches and apples." In *Environmental Toxicology and Chemistry*, Donald G. Crosby adds that "stone fruit pits, apple seeds, and lima beans are especially rich in cyanogenic glycosides [hydrogen cyanide compounds]," as are pear seeds, and he goes on to relate "the fatal poisoning of a man who ate a handful of... apple seeds he had saved for a treat."

Physics professor Brian H. Kaye, author of *Science and the Detective*, is in complete agreement: "Apple seeds...contain small amounts of cyanide compounds." He claims that "for this reason, there are no orchards in the gardens of prisons or mental institutions." Authors Cherie Calbom and Maureen Keane echo this warning in *Juicing for Life*. Since "apple seeds contain some cyanide," they recommend removing the seed of the fruit before juicing.

Toxicological Chemistry and Biochemistry author Stanley E. Manahan claims that much like the African tribal use of the calabar bean, "the Romans used cyanide from natural seed sources, such as apple seeds, for executions and suicides."

However, no need to panic if you do accidentally swallow a couple of seeds! Howard Hillman in *The New Kitchen Science* points out that "the quantity of cyanide in the seeds is minute." Accidentally swallowing an occasional seed is not a concern, but please don't munch them on purpose (Mother!).

SPROUTED AND GREEN POTATOES ARE POISONOUS

THE POTATO IS A MEMBER OF THE SOLANACEAE FAMILY, WHICH includes tomatoes and deadly nightshade. Potato and tomato plants contain toxins but, as Professor Ian Shaw reassures us in *Is It Safe to Eat?*, "They are usually at nontoxic concentrations in the parts of the plants that we eat." However, light prompts both greening (caused by chlorophyll) and the production of these toxins. Even though the two processes are unconnected, one can be an indication of the other. Shaw warns that "levels of glycoalkaloids [toxins] in green potatoes can be very high indeed." *Food Chemical Composition* author Tim Hutton explains that "given the scope for confusion, it is best to assume that green potatoes will contain high levels of glycoalkaloids."

Glycoalkaloids can cause severe illness. *Naturally Occurring Glycosides* (edited by Raphael Ikan) details an early study with prisoners in which six volunteers (it's good to know they offered to be poisoned) developed nausea and diarrhea after eating potatoes containing glycoalkaloids. M. McMillan and J. C. Thompson's 1979 report—"An Outbreak of Suspected Solanine Poisoning in Schoolboys," published in the *Quarterly Journal of Medicine*—relates how schoolboys were accidentally poisoned by toxic potatoes "left in the stores since the summer term." They recovered, but some needed hospital treatment. McMillan and Thompson reported that the remaining uncooked potatoes contained "about 330 milligrams per kilogram of glycoalkaloids...toxicity...similar to that of strychnine." Compared with that, modern-day school dinners seem almost acceptable.

Shaw estimates that death could occur from eating two

pounds of green potato skins or three pounds of potato sprouts, but warns that a smaller dose, while it may not prove fatal, could cause "a tummy upset." Hutton advises, "Handle raw potatoes with care and avoid bruising or other physical damage." He also recommends avoiding potatoes that have been damaged, poorly stored, or stressed during growing and harvesting. (There, there, potato. Go into the nice brown bag.)

It appears that the adage about avoiding eating green potato chips is also true. Shaw warns that "skin-on chips originating from green potatoes can have enough glycoalkaloid in two standard packets to result in toxicity in children."

ALWAYS DRINK MILK TO COUNTERACT THE HEAT IN SPICY FOOD, NEVER WATER

LAST CHRISTMAS, MY NIECE AND nephew devised a game of chocolate Russian roulette. The game unfolded much as you would imagine, with one of the chocolates filled with red-hot chili paste. (Far be it from me to criticize how young folk enjoy themselves these days.) My first thought was: Now's my chance to test the water-versus-milk theory. Actually, that was my second thought. My first thought was: I hope I don't get the red-hot chili-paste chocolate.

Suffice it to say I didn't get the chocolate, but the theory holds good. In *The Recipe Writer's Handbook*, authors Barbara Gibbs Ostmann and Jane L. Baker explain that the hot component in chilies, capsaicin, dissolves in fat-based liquids but not in water, and this is why milk reduces the heat in your mouth "more readily." Kerry K. Karukstis and Gerald R. Van Hecke in *Chemistry Connections* give a little more detail, explaining that, for example, "salt dissolves readily in water, while…many 'hot' spices [including constituents of ginger, white and black pepper, paprika, and chili peppers]…dissolve only partially in water." However, they are soluble in alcohol, oils, and fats. Karukstis and Van Hecke recommend fat-based accompaniments such as "sour cream or a beverage containing some alcohol" to alleviate the burning sensation on the pain receptors in the mouth. It would appear, therefore, that the tradition of washing down Mexican food with a few Margaritas is grounded in hard science. However, I furnished my unlucky mother, who had the misfortune to bite into the chili-filled chocolate, with a nice glass of milk and that also did the trick.

FROZEN VEGETABLES ARE JUST AS NUTRITIOUS AS FRESH ONES

MANY PEOPLE DISMISS THE HUMBLE BAG OF FROZEN VEGETABLES AS inferior to fresh, yet in *Counselling for Eating Disorders* Sara Gilbert states that frozen vegetables are "just as nutritious as fresh ones." In *Staying Healthy with Nutrition*, Dr. Elson M. Haas agrees that "frozen vegetables, when they are frozen fresh, have not suffered much loss of nutrients and may be kept for quite a long time, remaining nutritionally rich."

It's true to say that you probably can't beat produce from your local farmer's market, but if you are buying green beans in December it's very likely that they have traveled quite some dis-

tance to arrive on your dinner table, and they will therefore be depleted in nutrients. *Cooking Basics* (edited by Robert Norton) informs us that "there are many vegetables (peas, broad beans, sliced runner beans) that are usually better bought frozen than what is laughably called fresh."

Ironically, it isn't how the vegetables are preserved, but the length and method of cooking that has the greatest impact on their nutrient content. Gilbert gives valuable advice for preserving vegetable nutrients: "Do not overcook vegetables, as this reduces their vitamin content." It is considered much better to "cook in a small amount of boiling water for the shortest possible time." Norton suggests that frozen summer fruits like raspberries and currants are also well worth considering, and they are usually much less expensive when bought frozen.

THE BANANA TREE IS A GIANT HERB

CULTIVATED MAINLY IN THE ISLANDS OF THE ATLANTIC AND PACIFIC, "banana" is the fruit's Guinean name. In *An A-Z of Food and Drink* (edited by John Ayto), it is suggested that this word might derive from the Arabic *banana*, meaning "finger, toe." In *Regional Survey of the World: South America, Central* 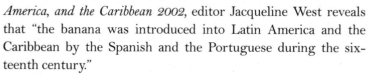 *America, and the Caribbean 2002*, editor Jacqueline West reveals that "the banana was introduced into Latin America and the Caribbean by the Spanish and the Portuguese during the sixteenth century."

Dennis N. Fox states in *Totally Bananas* that "no one knows with certainty when the first banana arrived on United States shores." But Fox claims that the honor of importing it lies with "an unnamed merchantman [who] delivered the first shipment probably from Panama, to Salem, Massachusetts, in 1690." Fox also quotes seventeenth-century Puritans who were the first to try the exotic fruit. They boiled the banana with pork and reported that it "tasted like soap." (Perhaps they neglected to peel it.)

The banana certainly comes from tropical treelike plants, but the *Encyclopaedia Britannica* reveals that it is "a gigantic herb that springs from an underground stem or rhizome." M. K. Smith and colleagues, whose treatise is included in *Biotechnology of Fruit and Nut Crops*, explain that bananas and plantains have large false trunks "composed of tightly clasping leaf sheaths." Each plant produces only one bunch of fruit, after which it is felled. Underground "suckers" then shoot up to replace the spent parent plant, and so the cycle continues. M. K. Smith points out that the banana "has the distinction of being the largest herb in the world," whose "pseudostems" can reach "up to fifteen feet." Try growing that on your windowsill!

BIRD'S NEST SOUP IS MADE FROM BIRDS' NESTS

YOU'LL BE GLAD TO HEAR THAT IT'S NOT JUST ANY OLD NEST THAT goes into the Chinese delicacy bird's nest soup. In *The Bird Almanac*, the aptly named David M. Bird defines the delicacy as "Asian or Chinese soup made from saliva used by certain swiftlets to cement their nests." That excellent volume *The Oxford Companion to Food* adds that "contrary to popular belief, the bird's nests are not found in the faces of cliffs, but in caves." The gathering of said nests is a dangerous and slippery business, which thus makes nests highly prized by Chinese-food gourmets. They cost around $2,000 per pound, which means that one large nest might sell for at least $400.

The *Companion* explains further that the swiftlets make their nests by cementing "a scaffolding of tiny twigs together with a sticky substance, which has been variously identified as coming from regurgitated seaweed such as agar-agar." It adds that it could simply be "the birds' own saliva." This has given rise to the debate as to whether bird's nest soup is of vegetable or animal origin, but the problem is that the nests are just too expensive to justify analytical research on them. Surely there must be someone out there willing to find out for certain, and hang the expense!

It's not a problem for me, since I doubt I shall be sampling them. The Eastern delicacy is off-white with a jellylike texture when cooked, and is said to taste "rubbery" to a Western palate. Mmmm—sounds delightful....

CHAPTER 6

Royalty Through *the* Ages

FOURTEENTH-CENTURY KING RICHARD II MARRIED A SEVEN-YEAR-OLD

IN 1377 KING RICHARD II SUCCEEDED TO THE ENGLISH THRONE AGED just ten. He was married at fifteen to Anne of Bohemia and widowed by the age of twenty-seven. He was, by all accounts, grief-stricken, but his new status did give him the opportunity to cement a useful foreign alliance by making a second royal marriage. The successful candidate was Isabella of Valois, the daughter of King Charles VI of France, who was just seven years old. When the extreme youth of his betrothed was pointed out, King Richard's response, as recorded in *Lives of the Queens of England* by Agnes and Elisabeth Strickland, was, "Every day would remedy the deficiency of age," and that at the age of twenty-seven he was "young enough to wait for her."

Charles VI was equally keen to secure an alliance with the English throne by marrying Isabella to Richard. According to medieval-history professor Nigel Saul, writing in *Richard II*, Richard promised that he would "take another of her father's close relatives in marriage if she died before she was thirteen"— his granddaughter, perhaps?

In *A Survay* [Survey] *of London: Contayning the Originall, Antiquity, Increase, Moderne Estate, and Description of That Citie,* written in 1598, sixteenth-century historian John Stow explains, not surprisingly, that "the young queen Isabella, [was] commonly called the Little (for she was not eight years old)." The English populace was so eager to see "the Little Queen" that upon her arrival "on London Bridge nine persons were crushed to death."

In *Studies in the Literary Imagination,* history author Rossell Hope Robbins suggests that Chaucer's 1396 poem "To Rosemounde" (rose of the world) may have been addressed to

Isabella, having been inspired by one of her wedding trousseau dresses, which was embroidered with pearl roses.

The King wed his young bride in November 1396. No children would come from the marriage, possibly because Richard was too busy with his favorites Michael de la Pole and Robert de Vere, but more likely because they were still waiting for Isabella to reach puberty. Sadly, though, the Little Queen wasn't destined to be queen for long. In February 1400 she was widowed at the tender age of ten when Richard died at the hands of his usurper, Henry Bolingbroke (later Henry

IV). She eventually returned to France where, aged eighteen, she married her twelve-year-old cousin, the Duc d'Orléans. She died in childbirth aged twenty-one, after having suffered what appears to be a lifelong case of *noblesse oblige.*

Another youthful Queen Isabella of England was Isabella of

Angoulême, who became the consort of thirty-three-year-old King John in August 1200, when she was twelve or thirteen.

QUEEN VICTORIA'S HUSBAND PRINCE ALBERT HAD A GENITAL PIERCING

THE PIERCING OF THE MALE MEMBER IS TERMED a "Prince Albert," named after Queen Victoria's faithful consort. But surely this respectable Victorian prince didn't embrace the art of body piercing? That reliable tome *The Oxford Companion to the Body* (edited by Colin Blakemore) laments that due to the nature of the practice being hidden by clothing "it is virtually impossible to write a history of piercing." Yet the volume goes on to reveal that "it is said that the genital piercing, the 'Prince Albert,' originated at the Victorian court, where it was used to attach the penis discreetly to the inside leg of male courtiers."

According to Marilee Strong, author of *A Bright Red Scream: Self-Mutilation and the Language of Pain* (which is a fascinating book, despite its scary title), "nipple and genital piercing was considered quite fashionable among British royalty during the Victorian era." At the time, male legwear was close-fitting, similar to modern-day cycle pants, and so untidiness in the breeches would have been all too evident. Strong confirms that the piercing reportedly allowed the Prince "to tether his penis to his leg, in order to fit into the tight pants that were the fashion of the day."

This practice doesn't, as some have imagined, reveal a secret salacious side to Prince Albert. He remains one hundred percent stuffy. The piercing was solely a practical measure designed to achieve sartorial streamlining of the breeches.

QUEEN CLEOPATRA PRESENTED HERSELF TO CAESAR WRAPPED IN CARPET OR BEDDING

AT THE AGE OF EIGHTEEN, FIRST–CENTURY B.C. Cleopatra Thea Philopator became the coruler of Egypt along with her twelve-year-old brother, Ptolemy XIII, whom she was obliged to marry in 51 B.C. After their union she took the name Cleopatra VII.

Keeping it in the family didn't do Cleopatra much good, however, as disputes between the two siblings arose, and about three years later her brother-husband's advisers ousted her from power. Not one to take kindly to such treatment, Cleopatra set out to appeal to Roman ruler Julius Caesar for reinstatement.

In *Cleopatra*, biographer Michael Grant claims that the story of Sicilian merchant Apollodorus smuggling Cleopatra past the coast guard "in a carpet or a roll of bedding" may well be true. First-century C.E. Greek historian and biographer Plutarch gives more details in *The Life of Julius Caesar*. (In *Plutarch and the Historical Tradition*, Philip Stadter informs us that Plutarch's writings are based on "the account of Cleopatra's physician" and so should prove reasonably accurate.) Plutarch writes that "Cleopatra, taking only Apollodorus the Sicilian from among her friends, embarked in a little skiff and landed at the palace when it was already getting dark ... she stretched herself at full length inside a bed-sack, while Apollodorus tied the bed-sack up with a cord and carried it indoors to Caesar." Plutarch explains that it probably wasn't showmanship that prompted the Egyptian queen to arrive in this manner: It would have been dangerous for Cleopatra to have been seen, and using standard means of entrance would have made it "impossible to escape notice."

However, the unusual entrance appears to have worked in her favor, since, according to Plutarch, "it was by this device of Cleopatra's, it is said, that Caesar was first captivated, for she showed herself to be a bold coquette." Julius Caesar then succumbed "to the charm of further intercourse with her," and who can blame him, when his initial impression was probably that some tiresome well-wisher had sent him yet another bedroll.

SIR WALTER RALEIGH LAID HIS CLOAK OVER A PUDDLE FOR QUEEN ELIZABETH I TO STEP UPON

THIS TALE ABOUT SIXTEENTH-CENTURY ADVENTURER SIR WALTER Raleigh is often dismissed as untrue. Some modern historians doubt the word of seventeenth-century preacher and historical author Thomas Fuller, who described the incident most eloquently in *The Worthies of England*, which was published posthumously in 1663: "This Captain Raleigh, coming out of Ireland to the English Court in good habit (his clothes being then a considerable part of his estate), found the Queen walking, till, meeting with a splashy place she seemed to scruple going thereon." Fuller goes on to reveal that "Presently, Raleigh cast and spread his new plush coat on the ground, whereon the Queen trod gently, rewarding him afterwards with many *suits*, for his so free and seasonable tender of so fair a footcloth." The event is also recorded in *Sir Walter Raleigh's History of the World* to which "An Account of the Author's Life, Tryal, and

Death" was added in 1687: "It was his Fortune one day to find the Queen walking abroad, who coming to a fenny place, there made a stop, the scrupling to tread thereon...."

The fact that Fuller tells the story so well is possibly his downfall and perhaps why he is accused of making it up. Victorian biographer Patrick Fraser Tytler, writing in his 1844 work *Life of Sir Walter Raleigh*, claims that "the anecdote...almost proves itself to be true by the knowledge it evinces Raleigh to have possessed of the character of Elizabeth." In other words, Raleigh would have calculated that precisely this sort of act would be the very thing to impress the vain and flirty Queen Elizabeth. In *Sir Walter Raleigh and His Times*, Charles Kingsley agrees that "it is very likely to be a true story."

CHAPTER 7

Famous Historical Figures

SCIENCE GENIUS ALBERT EINSTEIN
WAS EXPELLED FROM SCHOOL

ALBERT EINSTEIN IS CONSIDERED TO HAVE HAD ONE OF THE GREATEST minds of the twentieth century. Indeed, his very name has become synonymous with genius. It is therefore surprising to learn that, according to the *Encyclopaedia Britannica*, Einstein initially "showed little scholastic ability." Furthermore, in *Variety in Science History*, Vararadaraja V. Raman reveals that Einstein was "expelled from the Luitpold Gymnasium [Interdenominational School] in Munich." *Britannica* also confirms that in 1894, at the age of fifteen, Einstein left school with "poor grades" and "no diploma."

His family then moved to Italy, and Einstein's higher education continued in Switzerland. As Ze'ev Rosenkranz explains in *The Einstein Scrapbook*, after a brief time spent at a school in Aarau, Einstein attended the Federal Polytechnic Academy in Zurich from 1896 to 1900, where he studied until he was twenty-one. In *Einstein's Mirror*, Tony Hey and Patrick Walters describe how the great man's mathematics professor, Hermann Minkowski, "believed Einstein to be a 'lazy dog' since the young man showed little interest in mathematics and only occasionally bothered to attend his lectures." Stephanie Sammartino McPherson, in her biographical work *Albert Einstein*, quotes him as rather modestly claiming that "I am neither especially clever nor especially gifted. I am only very, very curious."

Einstein's scholastic problems certainly weren't associated with low intelligence, however. Raman points out that by the time he had reached higher education, "the exceptional keenness of his mind became very apparent." Yet, in *The Psychology of Abilities, Competencies, and Expertise*, editors Robert J. Sternberg and Elena Grigorenko reveal that "Einstein was able to pass his [polytechnic]...examinations only with the help of a classmate, Marcel Grossmann." The volume adds that Einstein's "academic performance was insufficient to enable him to secure a regular academic position," and after a two-month temporary teaching post in a school in Schaffhausen, Rosenkranz reports that he finished up working as a "technical expert third class" in the Swiss Patent Office in Bern in 1902. When Einstein later became successful, therefore, his former teacher Minkowski commented, "Oh, that Einstein, always cutting lectures—I really would not have believed him capable of it."

Throughout his schooldays, Einstein had failed to apply himself to his schoolwork. Dean Keith Simonton, writing in *Creativity in Science*, offers some insight into the reason, revealing that Einstein complained that modern methods of instruction were apt to strangle "the holy curiosity of enquiry." He felt strongly that the enjoyment of seeking and searching could not be promoted by "coercion and a sense of duty." Einstein found cramming for exams so counterproductive to his creative thinking that he stated it had made "scientific problems distasteful to me for an entire year." The educational system, it would appear, was "curing" Einstein of his enthusiasm for learning.

Albert Einstein did indeed have a poor academic record, but it would seem that it was due to the lack of flexibility in the educational system rather than flaws in his intelligence.

CHARLES DARWIN, CREATOR OF THE THEORY OF EVOLUTION, MARRIED HIS FIRST COUSIN

NINETEENTH–CENTURY NATURAL HISTORIAN Charles Darwin may have given early acknowledgment to the importance of genetics in natural selection, but genetics didn't seem to be an issue when he chose a wife.

In *The Correspondence of Charles Darwin* (Volume 2, 1837–43), Darwin penciled a list under the title "This is the Question." He then headed two columns "Marry" and "Not Marry." In the "Marry" column he listed the pluses: "constant companion . . . who will feel interest in one, object to be beloved & played with—better than a dog anyhow." Darwin also valued the "Charms of music and female chitchat" as "good for one's health—*but* [a] *terrible loss of time.*" However, he did console himself with the prospect of "a nice soft wife on a sofa with a good fire. . . ."

In the "Not Marry" column, top of the list came: "Not forced to visit relatives, & to bend in every trifle." Darwin was also concerned about having "less money for books &c" and not being able to "read in the Evenings." He was also concerned that, should his wife dislike London, "then the sentence is banishment & degradation into indolent, idle fool—"

Darwin decided, despite the many drawbacks, to "Marry—Marry—Marry Q.E.D." He may not have been able to head off the time-wasting female chitchat entirely, but by proposing to his first cousin Emma, he cleverly avoided gaining more relations to visit. The history books are silent upon precisely how the Darwins spent their evenings, but their marriage did result in ten children, which would strongly suggest that they eventually hit upon some form of mutually rewarding occupation.

EIGHTEENTH-CENTURY AUSTRIAN COMPOSER MOZART WAS BURIED IN A MASS GRAVE

WOLFGANG AMADEUS MOZART (HIS BAPTISMAL MIDDLE NAME WAS Theophilus, which means "lover of God" in Greek, but he preferred the Latinized version, Amadeus) was a musical child prodigy, but at just thirty-five years of age he succumbed to what, at the time, was certified as "rheumatic inflammatory fever." The *Encyclopaedia Britannica* reveals that Mozart was "buried in a multiple grave." It is regularly suggested in biographies of Mozart and elsewhere that this "pauper's grave" burial was due to poverty and was an ignominious end to a great man's life. However, *Britannica* contradicts this commonly held belief with the explanation that this type of burial was "standard at the time in Vienna for a person of his [Mozart's] social and financial situation."

Indeed, in *Notes on Mozart*, biographer Conrad Wilson points out that "the communal grave into which his body was lowered...carried no social stigma for which Vienna could be posthumously blamed." Wilson goes on to explain that "it was simply the form of the burial—hygienic and space-saving—recommended at the time by the Emperor and encouraged by the city's authorities." Rob Humphreys confirms this assertion in *The Rough Guide to Vienna*, and adds an interesting detail explaining that due to reforms brought in by Joseph II, "mass burials were the rule; only the very wealthy could afford to have a family vault, and attending of individual graves was virtually unknown."

Mozart's burial, then, was no different from that of most people in Vienna in that era. According to Humphreys, it was only during the mid-nineteenth century that the Viennese taste turned to lavish funeral services and impressive monuments. And only then did it become "a scandal" that no one knew where Mozart was buried. In the nineteenth century, the people of Vienna rectified this by having a monument erected on the approximate site of Mozart's grave. The monument incorporates a mourning angel and a broken pillar, the latter symbolizing Mozart's early demise. So although his death may have been untimely, his burial was perfectly respectable.

VIOLET JESSOP, WHO SAILED ON THE *TITANIC* AND THE *BRITANNIC*, SURVIVED BOTH SINKINGS

VIOLET JESSOP WAS A STEWARDESS FOR THE WHITE STAR LINE IN THE early 1900s. Her incredible story is described in her autobiographical work *Titanic Survivor*. Violet had an eventful association with three ill-fated White Star liners, which began with her serving on the *Olympic* in 1911. While she was on board, it collided with the British warship HMS *Hawke*. Both ships sustained damage, but no lives were lost.

The following year, Violet was traveling on the *Titanic* when it struck an iceberg and sank. Violet explains how, on viewing the terrible scene from the safety of a lifeboat, she watched the ship "give a lurch forward...she went down by the head with a thundering roar of underwater explosions, our proud ship, our beautiful *Titanic* gone to her doom."

In 1916, during the First World War, Violet was working as a Red Cross nurse aboard the *Britannic* when it also sank after

striking a naval mine. Violet describes being washed overboard and hit by the ship's propellers: "Just as life seemed nothing but a whirling, choking ache, I rose to the light of day, my nose barely above the little lapping waves...my life jacket was loose and not sufficient to support me. Just then another went floating by so I grabbed at it...at last I had something to hold on to."

Violet confides that "drowning was my one irrational fear all my life," which is not surprising really (and hardly irrational) when one considers her life history. She reveals that she "had not been able to learn to swim because of the loss of part of one lung." For a one-lunged nonswimmer with a sea-based career, it has to be said that she did pretty well. But with all that bad luck, I'm not sure I'd have wanted to sail with her.

MICHAEL JACKSON TRIED TO PURCHASE THE SKELETON OF THE ELEPHANT MAN

THE "ELEPHANT MAN" WAS THE BYNAME OF JOSEPH CAREY MERRICK (sometimes inaccurately referred to as John Merrick). He was born physically deformed due to a severe combination of what was believed to be neurofibromatosis and Proteus syndrome. After a brief career as a professional "freak," he was discovered by a London physician, Frederick Treves, and became a patient of the Royal London Hospital, Whitechapel, in 1886. He remained there until 1890, when, at the age of twenty-seven, he died in his sleep of accidental suffocation. Merrick's preserved skeleton is held at the hospital, although it is not on general view to the public.

A rumor persists that Michael Jackson attempted to purchase the skeleton from the Royal London Hospital in 1987. In *Michael Jackson: The Solo Years*, biographers Craig Halstead and Chris Cadman reveal that in a 1993 television interview with Oprah Winfrey "Michael angrily denounced the...Elephant Man stories." In *Freakery: Cultural Spectacles of the Extraordinary Body* (edited by Rosemarie G. Thomson), it is explained that "Jackson told Oprah Winfrey that it was just 'another stupid story. Where am I gonna put some bones, and why would I want them?'"

However, it appears that Jackson's then manager, Frank Dileo, made an offer on Jackson's behalf for the remains of Joseph Merrick. Jonathan Evans, trust archivist for the Royal London Hospital, offered the following clarification: "I can confirm that we hold a Medical College Secretary's correspondence file 1980–90...which includes a letter dated April 24, 1987 from Frank Dileo, Artist Management Inc." Evans went on to reveal that "the letter makes an offer for the skeleton of Joseph Merrick, which was part of the Pathology Museum collection of the Medical College." He concluded that "the Medical College replied on May 28, 1987, refusing the offer. The file also contains several newspaper clippings dating from May 29, 1987, onwards in which Mr. Dileo is quoted as talking about the story."

It's a mystery as to why Jackson has been so coy about the attempted purchase. Details from a Los Angeles press release dated May 29 stated that he "hopes to add them [the remains] to his collection of rare and unusual memorabilia at his California compound" and "cares about and is concerned with the Elephant Man as a dedicated and devoted collector of art and antiques." Other commentators on the subject have since dismissed the offer as a publicity stunt, and so it would appear that the truth behind the singer's interest in the Elephant Man's unique remains might never be properly uncovered.

Food *and* Drink History

OYSTERS WERE THE FOOD OF THE POOR

NOWADAYS, OYSTERS ARE considered a rare and luxurious delicacy to be savored raw on the half shell, but in years gone by it wasn't always so. In fact, *The Oxford Companion to Food* explains that well into the middle of the nineteenth century "oysters were plentiful and cheap in both Britain and North America." Dishes such as oyster stews and soups, fried oysters, oysters on skewers with bits of bacon, and oyster fritters were common.

In *Oyster*, literary historian Rebecca Stott reveals that oysters were once so plentiful in America that they were "eaten by Native

Americans...and...used to trade with inland tribes." Indeed, Stott quotes late-seventeenth-century settlers in Maryland complaining to British authorities that because their provisions were in such short supply, to keep from starving they were obliged to "eat the oysters taken from along their shores." Stott surmises that "from such accounts it seems that...oysters were seen as a subsistence food associated with the eating customs of the natives, not a delicacy for 'civilized' settlers."

A similar rags-to-riches food is salmon. Regarded as a luxury food in modern times, in the nineteenth century—as revealed in Nancy Lord's *Fishcamp: Life on an Alaskan Shore*—"the long-departed Atlantic salmon...once had been so plentiful and cheap that Massachusetts colonists were forbidden to feed it to their servants more than once a week." Even more surprisingly, perhaps, in *The Taste of American Place*, edited by geography professors Barbara G. and James R. Shortridge, we learn that lobster was regarded by New Englanders as "cheap, low-status—even poorhouse—fare." The volume explains that "lobsters were many times donated to widows, orphans, and others in the spirit of public charity." Indeed "so devalued were they as a food source that there are reports of saltwater farmers gathering them in carts after storms...and either feeding them to the pigs or plowing them by the ton into their rocky fields as fertilizer." It was with the advent of more efficient transport that it became lucrative to transport lobsters to other parts of the country and only then did they start their climb to luxury status.

CANNED FOOD CAN LAST A HUNDRED YEARS

THERE ARE QUITE A FEW ANCIENT CANS OF FOOD IN MY CUPBOARD, IN particular a can of processed meat I bought in error and certainly have no intention of eating. I don't think it's reached its centenary yet, but if it had it is quite possible it would still be edible (or at least as edible as it ever was). From *A Short History of Technology* by T. K. Derry and Trevor I. Williams, we learn that the preserving process was invented in 1795 by a Parisian confectioner, Nicolas Appert, in order to keep food edible for the French army.

In *Packaging, Policy and the Environment*, Geoffrey M. Levy reveals that "Appert sold the English version of his patent to... [British merchant] Peter Durand, who was the first to suggest the use of metal canisters, which were lighter and less fragile than glass." In 1810, Durand patented the use of tin-coated iron cans. J.A.G. Rees explains in *Processing and Packaging of Heat Preserved Foods* that in America, in 1819, English immigrant William Underwood "opened a factory in Boston preserving fruit, pickles and sauces." The volume also reveals that "Thomas Kensett set up a similar factory in New York." Both Underwood and Kensett initially used glass jars and cork stoppers as Appert had done.

By 1820 Durand was supplying canned food to the Royal Navy. Levy adds that the first "patented preserved meats" were tested on "sick sailors." This provision was called "canned soup and *bouilli* [meat stew]," but the British sailors preferred to refer to it using a more familiar term for pickled beef dating back to the eighteenth century: "bully beef." Rees states that during the American Civil War there was additional increase in demand for canned food, as well as for "vital stores" carried by wagon trains "in the expansion of the West."

And as for the content of a can being able to last more than a hundred years, *The Oxford Companion to Food* recounts how two cans—"one of veal and one of carrots"—originally made for an Arctic expedition of 1824 were opened 114 years later by curious scientists. The contents were in "sound condition, only slightly spoiled by the slow chemical attack of the tin coating." Apparently, the veal and carrots "could have been eaten safely," but the investigators declined to sample them.

The can opener wasn't invented until around fifty years after the creation of the tin can, but this fact doesn't seem quite so odd when one considers that canned food was still largely confined to army rations, and the soldiers were expected to open their cans without recourse to namby-pamby labor-saving devices. As *Tin and Its Uses* (produced by the National Tin Research and Development Council) points out, the legend printed on the label of an 1824 can of roast veal simply stated: "Cut round the top with a hammer and chisel." During the American Civil War, Jack Coggins claims in *Arms and Equipment of the Civil War*, the bayonet was seldom used as a weapon and served mainly as a "can opener, [and] roasting spit."

When canned food became available to the public in 1830, shopkeepers were obliged to open the cans for their customers in the store, which rather defeated the object of buying preserved goods. Finally, as Ian Harrison reveals in *The Book of Inventions*, it was an Englishman, cutler and surgical instrument-maker Robert Yeates, who, in 1855, invented the can opener, for "improvements applicable to lock knives and lever knives, partly applicable to such surgical and other instruments as may be connected to handles by moving joints." Essentially, this was a penknife, with "blades that folded into the handle...such lever knife being a curved blade with a shoulder...forming an efficient bearing or fulcrum in use."

As a child, I recall watching—with a mixture of horror and delight—as my normally sedate grandmother viciously hacked the tops off cans with just such a billhook-style instrument.

Thank goodness for the invention of less noisy devices, and indeed for the humble pull tab, which renders even the most sophisticated of can openers redundant in the modern world.

NINETEENTH-CENTURY COCA-COLA CONTAINED COCAINE

THE INSPIRATION FOR COCA–COLA CAME from the popular mid-nineteenth-century, coca-leaf-based wine Vin Mariani. Writing in *Murder, Magic & Medicine,* chemistry professor John Mann explains that this beverage even won testimonials from "Queen Victoria and...the Vatican under Pope Leo XIII." It's true that coca leaves contain the alkaloid cocaine, but as biology professor John Kricher explains in *A Neotropical Companion,* such leaves contain "only one percent cocaine." Furthermore, as David T. Courtwright adds in an essay printed in *Consuming Habits: Drugs in History and Anthropology,* Vin Mariani was a "comparatively mild product" compared to the modern-day crack cocaine developed in the 1980s.

The *Encyclopaedia Britannica* tells how, in 1886, U.S. pharmacist John S. Pemberton devised an alcohol-free concoction based on "cocaine from the coca leaf and caffeine-rich extracts of the kola nut." *Cassell's Dictionary of Word Histories* confirms that the drink was "flavored with coca leaves [and] cola nuts." *Britannica* goes on to explain that Pemberton "originally touted his drink as a tonic for most common ailments," while *The Oxford English Dictionary* tells how the Atlanta *Evening Journal* of 1887 proclaimed: "Drink the brain tonic and intellectual soda fountain beverage Coca-Cola."

Professor Richard Isralowitz, writing in *Drug Use, Policy and Management*, claims that "the unique shape of the Coca-Cola bottle was intended to resemble the shape of the coca bean." However, the designer got things rather muddled and the bottle finished up shaped like a cocoa bean instead!

Soon, various cola drinks were being manufactured as health elixirs. Paul E. Lovejoy, in an essay included in *Consuming Habits*, states that "Caleb D. Bradham, a North Carolina pharmacist, created…Pepsi-Cola" by combining "sugar, vanilla, oils, spices and kola." Like Coca-Cola, it was advertised as a medical tonic, but was said to "relieve dyspepsia (upset stomach) and peptic ulcers"—hence the name.

At the beginning of the twentieth century, the addictive properties of cocaine were recognized, and *Britannica* assures us that "the cocaine was removed from Coca-Cola's formula in 1905." *Medical Toxicology* authors E. Martin Caravati and Michael A. McCuigan agree, revealing that in the early 1900s "the cocaine in Coca-Cola was replaced with caffeine." Indeed, Isralowitz claims that in 1909, the Food and Drug Administration made "charges against the [Coca-Cola] company" stating that "it was misbranded because it contained 'no coca and little if any cola.'" By this time, Coca-Cola had become a recognized brand, known by the public to be cocaineless, so the charge of misbranding was rejected and the name was retained.

During the twentieth century, Coca-Cola, the popular soft drink, then grew into what *Britannica* describes as an American "cultural institution."

***

THE PILGRIMS LANDED AT PLYMOUTH ROCK BECAUSE THEY HAD RUN OUT OF BEER

THIS FUN TALE SOUNDS NO MORE THAN AN AMUSING LEGEND, BUT IT'S founded in truth. In 1620, English pilgrims hired seamen to transport them by ship to the New World. In *Everyday Life in Colonial America*, Dale Taylor reveals that one major reason why the Pilgrims landed at Massachusetts instead of continuing on to the latitude of their charter was due to "a shortage of beer."

Author of *Libations of the Eighteenth Century* David A. Woolsey quotes Governor Bradford of the Plymouth Plantation complaining that his settlers "were hastened ashore and made to drink water that the seamen might have more beer." In *The American Brewery: From Colonial Evolution to Microbrew Revolution*, Bill Yenne adds that once their passengers had been disembarked, the crew "headed home, keeping the beer that remained."

This wasn't, as it would first appear, so that the crew had the pleasure of a few beers for the journey home—it was simply a matter of survival. As Glenn A. Knoblock and James T. Gunter explain in *Brewing in New Hampshire*, at that time "beer was the universal beverage of Englishmen and not just due to matters of taste," since in England "water was often unfit for drinking." Plentiful supplies of fluid were essential for sea voyaging, so no beer on board meant no fluid. The crew were obliged to ration sufficient beer for the journey home if they wanted to avoid running short.

The newly disembarked Pilgrims found themselves in precisely the same parched predicament. One, Edward Winslow, writing in his 1622 work *Mourt's Relation: A Journal of the Pilgrims of Plymouth*, stated that when they landed they "marched through boughs and bushes…and yet could…[not] find any fresh water, which we greatly desired, and stood in need of, for we brought neither beer nor water with us…[and were] sore athirst." Eventually they found "springs of fresh water, of which we were heartily glad, and sat us down and drank our first New

England water with as much delight as ever we drank drink in all our lives."

Knoblock and Gunter agree that in the early days, the colonists would have been forced to drink water. However, in time, "the ingredients and means were found to brew beer and ale." They explain that "small beer" was the weakest beer in terms of alcoholic strength and was "meant to be consumed immediately after brewing." Such beer was first brewed in quantity "at Captain John Mason's Great House at Strawberry Banke," since in 1635 an inventory of his stores included "fifteen barrels of malt."

Nowadays, we use the term "small beer" to describe something of little importance; the very weakness of the beer is used to represent something of insignificance. Yet, ironically, "small beer" was clearly vital to life for seventeenth-century folk.

DRINKING COFFEE WAS ILLEGAL IN PARTS OF EUROPE IN THE SEVENTEENTH AND EIGHTEENTH CENTURIES

IN MID-SEVENTEENTH-CENTURY ENGLAND, DRINKING BEER ALL DAY was encouraged—it was coffee that was responsible for all the evils of the world. Eighteenth-century antiquarian-book collector William Oldys reports that a Mr. Edwards was responsible for the first London coffeehouse opening in 1652. Apparently, the trend started when Edwards's "Ragusan youth," whom he brought from Turkey "to prepare this drink for him every morning," was permitted to start selling it publicly. (This certainly brings a new dimension to the concept of traveling with one's own coffeemaker.) Coffeehouses soon began springing up throughout London, and by the start of

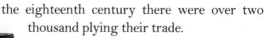

the eighteenth century there were over two thousand plying their trade.

At first, people approved of the new beverage. In 1657 the drink was said to "quickeneth the Spirits, [and] maketh the Heart lightsome." It was believed to be "good against Eyesores, Coughs and Colds, Rhumes, Consumptions, Headache, Dropsie, Gout, Scurvy" and many other complaints. In *Uncommon Grounds*, Mark Pendergrast quotes an English observer in 1674 commenting that "coffee-drinking hath caused the greatest sobriety among the nations." Apparently, before its introduction, "Apprentices and Clerks with others, used to take their morning's draft in Ale...which by the dizziness they cause in the Brain, make many unfit for business."

However, not everyone approved of the new fad. Unlike their continental counterparts, as Pendergrast explains, Englishwomen "were excluded from this all-male society." The Woman's Petition Against Coffee campaigned against "the Excessive use of that Newfangled, Abominable, Heathenish Liquor called Coffee," since they were finding "of late a very sensible Decay of that true Old English Vigour." Were they alluding to dissatisfaction in the bedroom? Yes, they were, as the petition clearly described: "Never did Men wear greater Breeches, or carry less in them of any mettle whatsoever."

Pendergrast reveals that in 1675, King Charles II issued a proclamation "for the suppression of coffee houses." A century later, Frederick the Great of Germany "forbad coffee's roasting except in official government establishments." In *J. S. Bach*, Albert Schweitzer reveals that during the eighteenth century many European princes expressly forbade the drinking of coffee.

In the seventeenth century, coffee made its appearance in the New World. In *The World of Caffeine*, Bonnie K. Bealer and Bennett Alan Weinberg reveal that the earliest reference to coffee-drinking in America dates back to New York in 1668. As in Europe, coffee began to replace beer "as the favorite breakfast beverage." In 1670, in Boston, one Dorothy Jones "was granted the first known license to sell coffee." Far from being rendered illegal, coffee actually became required drinking on patriotic grounds, since in 1773, opposition to British tax prompted the Boston Tea Party. This resulted in the British East India Company's cargoes of tea being jettisoned into Boston Harbor. Bealer and Weinberg claim that "from this moment in history, coffee became the favored caffeinated drink of the Americans, indispensable at the breakfast table and the workplace ever after."

Indeed, coffee became supremely important to the morale of soldiers in the mid-nineteenth century during the Civil War. Coffee was included in the official Federal ration, and in *Daily Life in Civil War America*, authors James M. and Dorothy Denneen Volo reveal that soldiers' diaries and letters were "full of relevant references to the hot brown liquid." However, the coffee was supplied in bean form and so "the soldier seized his musket by the barrel and used the butt as a tamper." The Volos quote an army surgeon stating that army coffee had "no equal as a prepara-

tion for a hard day's march, or any rival as restorative after one." This sentiment is heartily echoed by shoppers across the globe to this very day.

CHAPTER 9

Medical Matters

STARING AT THE SUN DURING AN ECLIPSE CAN CAUSE BLINDNESS

IN *THE PEDANT'S REVOLT*, I PASSED ON THE COMFORTING FACT THAT one can't easily blind oneself in everyday life. However, staring directly at the sun appears to be one way. *Sun Protection in Man*, edited by Paulo U. Giacomoni, contains a warning that "light...can do acute damage if it is sufficiently intense....Eyes can be damaged (temporarily or permanently)...from staring at the sun during an eclipse." This is also true of viewing the sun through apparatus. *The Cambridge Eclipse Photography Guide* author Michael A. Covington explains that looking at the sun through a camera or telescope without proper eye protection can "permanently damage our eyes." He points out that "this type of eye injury is usually painless," but within a few days it may develop into a "permanent blind spot." Ferenc Kuhn and Dante Pieramici, authors of *Ocular Trauma*, reveal that viewing through sunglasses or smoked glass doesn't offer effective protection either. In *A Textbook of*

Clinical Ophthalmology, Ronald Pitts Crick and colleagues explain that solar retinopathy (eclipse blindness) is caused by "visible light from an intense source such as the sun," which can result in "a focal retinal burn." Kuhn and Pieramici add that "there is no known therapy."

New Trends in Astronomy Teaching (edited by Gouguenheim, McNally, and Percy) sends out a clear message: "Never stare at the sun, not at an eclipse and not on a normal day." In a 2006 statement, the U.K.'s Department of Health states that its chief medical officer has noted that "a young boy suffered loss of central vision after looking directly at the  sun during a partial eclipse in October 2005." The statement, supported by the Royal Astronomical Society and the Royal College of Ophthalmologists, added that "permanent damage to the retina can occur without pain and the visual symptoms can be delayed for several hours."

CLOSE CONTACT WITH DOG FECES CAN CAUSE BLINDNESS

THERE ARE TWO POTENTIALLY SIGHT-DAMAGING PARASITES THAT are sometimes found in contaminated dog feces. The single-celled parasite *Toxoplasma gondii* can cause the disease toxoplasmosis, while the parasite *Toxocara canis* can lead to toxocariasis. Both can result in blindness.

Very few people infected with toxoplasmosis experience symptoms, because a healthy person's immune system usually keeps the parasite from causing illness. However, those who contract it with a weakened immune system can develop health problems such as swollen glands and fever. Toxoplasmosis can cause eye and brain damage to babies in the uterus.

James Serpell's work, *In the Company of Animals*, reveals that "humans can become infected with *Toxocara* through contact with soil contaminated with animal feces, or through direct contact with infected pets...in a small proportion of cases, the larvae migrate through the bloodstream and may lodge in the liver, the brain, the lungs, or in the back of the eye where they cause, respectively, liver enlargement, epilepsy, asthmalike respiratory problems, and impaired vision." In *Toxoplasmosis* (edited by David H. M. Joynson and Tim G. Wreghitt), the disease is described as "a significant and potentially fatal infection." The work states that fetal death can occur in "up to 2.2 percent" of infected women, and that "congenital toxoplasmosis is the cause of blind registration in 0.1–0.2 percent of patients." Though this may not be a large percentage, it is still of huge significance to the individuals concerned. Furthermore, S. L. Percival and colleagues explain in *Microbiology of Waterborne Diseases* that "the first recorded case of human toxoplasmosis was recognized retrospectively in an eleven-month-old infant with congenital hydrocephalus and microphthalmia."

Cat feces can also be a source of toxoplasmosis and toxocara infections. *Lecture Notes on Medical Microbiology* by Elliot, Hastings, and Desselberger reveals that "toxoplasmosis is a cause of glandular-fever syndrome. Infection in pregnancy may result in congenital toxoplasmosis, resulting in abortion or stillbirth." For this reason Dr. Leland S. Shapiro, writing in *Pathology & Parasitology for Veterinary Technicians*, recommends that "pregnant women should avoid being around cat feces, and eating rare meat like beef or pork." Shapiro goes on to recommend that "gardening with gloves and washing all fruit and vegetables (especially those grown organically) is strongly recommended." So, if you should fall over in the park and come to rest your hand in something brown and squashy, it's still an excellent idea to wash your hands thoroughly at your earliest convenience.

POPPY SEEDS CAN CAUSE A DRUG TEST TO READ POSITIVE

RANDOM DRUG–TESTING IS WIDESPREAD IN PROFESSIONAL SPORTS, IN the armed forces, and in some workplaces. False positives can occur with devastating results. In *The Great Drug War*, Arnold S. Trebach reveals that in a 1983 case "poppy seeds were the culprits when two Navy medical interns suddenly found themselves suspected of being morphine or heroin addicts." Trebach adds that the tests were repeated and produced the same results, and, unfortunately, both officers failed lie detector tests. Eventually, "Navy technicians discovered that both doctors liked the bagels topped with poppy seeds often served in the hospital cafeteria," and in fact it was those poppy seeds that "tested positive for morphine."

Indeed, G. L. Landry's 1994 research paper "False Positive Drug Test for Morphine: A Medical Detective Story," came to a similar conclusion. Dr. Steven B. Karch's *Drug Abuse Handbook* confirms this by stating that it is "not disputed that scientific literature on drug-testing reported ordinary poppy-seed consumption could produce positive test results for opiates." In *Karch's Pathology of Drug Abuse*, the author adds that "poppy-seed-containing pastries...cause positive urine tests for opiates." The reason is that "poppy seeds contain both morphine and codeine." Psychiatry professors David M. McDowell and Henry I. Spitz explain in *Substance Abuse* that poppy seeds contain "minute amounts of diacetyl-morphine [heroin]." However, "an individual would need to eat a substantial amount of the seeds to achieve a detectable level."

In *Encyclopedia of Security Management*, John Fay points out reassuringly that "the in-terfering substances are well-known to drug-testing laboratories and are easily resolved with alternative screening techniques." Karch adds that "although not yet offi-cially recognized, there are several...ways available to distin-guish narcotic abuse from poppy-seed ingestion." The *Textbook of Substance Abuse Treatment*, edited by Marc Galanter and Herbert D. Kleber, confirms that "positive laboratory results for opiates in urine tests are routinely reversed by medical review officers, mak-ing an opiate test of urine samples in the workplace all but worth-less because of the poppy-seed problem."

So, just how many poppy seeds need to be consumed to risk the unfortunate eventuality of testing positive to drugs? According to Dr. Karch the amount is "several teaspoons." One really would need to have some sort of bagel addiction to ingest that many, but clearly, it can happen.

CARROTS CAN TURN YOU ORANGE

THE CULPRIT IS THE PIGMENT CAROTENE, WHICH CAN TINT THE FAT layer under the skin a yellowy-orange color. The condition is called carotenodermia. *The Dietitian's Guide to Vegetarian Diets* (authored by Virginia Messina and colleagues) confirms it is "a benign condition...that can occur when large amounts of carotene-rich foods are ingested." As for the question "Doctor, why has my baby turned orange?," the answer can be found in

The Institute of Medicine's Dietary Reference Intakes for Vitamin C, Vitamin E, Selenium, and Carotenoids, where carotenodermia is revealed to be "the primary effect of excess carotenoid intake noted in infants, toddlers, and young children."

In *Laboratory Tests for the Assessment of Nutritional Status*, Howerde E. Sauberlich explains that "bronzing was observed in adult subjects over ninety days on a daily intake of approximately 30 milligrams of beta-carotene." This equated to about half a pound of carrots per day. However, Sauberlich reassures us that the condition "disappeared quickly" when the subjects stopped taking the supplements.

The word "bronzing" gives us a clue as to how these pigments have been marketed in the past. Carotenoids are sometimes included in so-called tanning pills. Of course, the pills don't tan, they tint, and unlike a true tan the pads of fat on the palms of hands and the soles of feet go particularly dark. Incidentally, the orange tinge also affects all bodily waste products.

Canthaxanthin, another tanning pigment, can lead to impaired vision, while one fatality due to aplastic anaemia has been attributed to tanning pills. If you fancy an even darker shade, Messina explains that lycopenodermia, a similar condition, is characterized by "deep orange discoloration of the skin" and can be developed by eating inordinate quantities of tomatoes.

Eating lots of carrots may turn you orange, but will you be compensated by being able to see in the dark? Only if you were deficient in carotene in the first place. In *From Dynasties to Dotcoms*, Carol Kennedy reveals that after the development of radar during the Second World War, "the [British] public was fed the propaganda story of 'night vision' among the fighter aces, aided by vitamin A," which is related to beta-carotene. The carrot-eating story was disseminated in an attempt to keep the extent of Britain's advances in radar secret. Kennedy recalls how countless children were encouraged to eat up their carrots thanks to the exploits of John "Cat's Eyes" Cunningham and his fellow night-fighter pilots. However, according to Kennedy, Cunningham attributed "all but one of his twenty enemy hits to radar." Beta-carotene in the guise of vitamin A can restore defective night vision, but excess vitamin A will not improve it beyond normal function.

MIXING HOUSEHOLD CLEANERS AND BLEACH CAN CAUSE IRREVERSIBLE LUNG DAMAGE

HOUSEHOLD CLEANING PRODUCTS CONTAINING AMMONIA COME IN the guise of wax removers and glass, window, oven, and bathroom cleaners. Vinegar is a popular alternative to these cleaners. Bleach is also a useful bathroom disinfectant, but, as the eponymous author of *Lewis' Dictionary of Toxicology* warns, "Never mix chlorine bleach with cleaning products containing ammonia, or with vinegar." The results could take your breath away—literally—since, as Lewis warns, "the resulting chloramine fumes are deadly." In *Chemistry Connections*, Kerry K. Karukstis and Gerald R. Van Hecke agree that "mixing bleach with cleaners containing ammonia leads to the formation of a family of potentially toxic compounds known as chloramines."

Phyllis Stoffman, author of *The Family Guide to Preventing and Treating 100 Infectious Illnesses*, explains further: "If you mix bleach with ammonia-containing compounds... dangerous gases are released. They can cause severe lung damage and pneumonia." She also warns against mixing "sodium hypochlorite (household bleach) with an acid [such as vinegar]... [since] chlorine gas and water are released." The chlorine gas then reacts with the water to form hydrochloric acid. Stoffman points out that "the gas and acid can cause serious symptoms ranging from eye irritation to dizziness, chest pain, and lung damage." These toxic gases have acrid fumes that can burn mucous (nose, throat, and lung) membranes. The pungent smell of this chemical reaction is similar to the chlorine odor of swimming pools, and is often mistaken for being simply that of household bleach. Furthermore, you can't even rely on the telltale smell to warn you, since scented bleaches can mask the whiff, so be vigilant when spring-cleaning.

ASPIRIN OCCURS NATURALLY IN THE BARK OF THE WILLOW TREE

THERE IS OFTEN A BIG DISTINCTION MADE BETWEEN "NATURAL" AND man-made remedies. The "natural" remedies are invariably perceived as being healthier. According to *Beneficial and Toxic Effects of Aspirin*, edited by Susan E. Feinman, "aspirin is the most extensively used therapeutic chemical in the world." Yet, it is not generally regarded as a "natural" remedy. H. Levesque's 2000 research paper "Aspirin Throughout the Ages: A Historical Review" explains that ancient civilizations as far back as "the Assyrians and the Egyptians were aware of the analgesic effects of a decoction of myrtle or willow leaves for joint pains." In *Chemistry: The Molecular Science*, Moore, Stanitski, and Jurs reveal that "nearly 2,500 years ago, the Greek physician Hippocrates recommended extracts of the bark of willow trees to alleviate the pain of childbirth." Sally S. Roach and Jeanne C. Scherer writing in *Introductory Clinical Pharmacology* add that in addition to its use as a pain reliever, "various species of willow bark and leaf have been used to lower fever and as an anti-inflammatory."

In *Electropharmacology* George M. Eckert explains how the Reverend Edward Stone wrote a letter to the president of the Royal Society in 1763 describing how he had tasted some willow bark from trees on his land and how "on finding it tasted bitter" he wondered if the bark might have "some of the effects of cinchona (which contains quinine)," which was used at the time to reduce fever and numb pain. Eckert then adds that in 1827 Frenchman Henri Leroux "extracted salicin from willow bark," and in 1838 Italian chemist Raffaele Piria "made salicylic acid [aspirin] from salicin."

Roach and Scherer suggest that "fewer adverse reactions are associated with willow bark than with salicylates." However, the natural compound present in willow bark can still cause adverse reactions for anyone who has an allergy to regular aspirin.

CHAPTER 10

The Human Body

MEN HAVE A HIGHER PAIN THRESHOLD THAN WOMEN

THE PALTRY PAIN THRESHOLD OF MEN IS OFTEN JOKED ABOUT, BUT clinical studies reveal a slightly different picture. In 1998, M. E. Robinson's research team tested men and women's sensitivity to pain. The resulting *Sex Differences in Clinical Pain: A Multisample Study* found "women reporting higher levels of clinical pain" than men. M. Unruh's 1996 study "Gender Variations in Clinical Pain Experience" also found that "in most studies, women report more severe levels of pain, more frequent pain and pain of longer duration than do men." The *Textbook of Cosmetic Dermatology* by Robert Baran and Howard I. Maibach confirms this, stating that in clinical tests, "women were more sensitive to small temperature changes and to pain caused by either heat or cold." The work points to anatomical differences in skin thickness as well as differences in blood flow and nerve structure as a possible explanation for the difference in pain perception. Given that women have, on

average, thinner skin than men, it would seem logical for them to feel pain stimuli sooner than men.

However, there may be another explanation for the reported difference: F. M. Levine and L. L. De Simone's 1991 study "The Effects of Experimenter Gender on Pain Report in Male and Female Subjects" found that "males reported significantly less pain in front of a female experimenter than a male experimenter." It should also be added that "experimenters were [deliberately] selected for their attractiveness." In S. MacIntyre's 1993 study "Gender Differences in the Perceptions of Common Cold Symptoms," "Volunteers assessed the presence and severity of colds at the end of their stay in the [Medical Research Council Common Cold] Unit." The study found that "men were significantly more likely to 'overrate' their symptoms in comparison with the clinical observer than were women." In *Essential Health Psychology*, senior lecturer in psychology Mark Forshaw suggests that this does not "contradict the work that shows that pain threshold and tolerance is lower in women, since common colds, like many illnesses, do not involve significant pain, but instead, a constellation of unpleasant bodily symptoms."

In the light of this fascinating theory, therefore, I suggest to all women that the next time a male relation comes down with a cold, why not enlist a stunning female friend or colleague to inquire, on your behalf, as to how he is feeling. A miracle recovery will be more or less guaranteed.

THE HYOID BONE IN THE THROAT IS NOT
ATTACHED TO ANY OTHER BONE

THE HORSESHOE-SHAPED HYOID BONE AT THE FRONT OF THE NECK, which serves as an anchoring structure for the tongue, is, according to the *Encyclopaedia Britannica*, the only bone in the human body that does not articulate with any other bone. It gets its name from the Greek word *hyoeides*, meaning "shaped like the [Greek] letter upsilon, which is shaped like a lowercase *u*." In *Basic Medical Science for Speech, Hearing and Language Students*, Martin Atkinson and Stephen McHanwell reveal that it is "attached by muscles, ligaments and membranes" to the jawbone, skull, and voice box. In *Anatomy and Physiology*, edited by Bonnie Roesch, it is revealed that "the single hyoid bone...is a unique component of the axial skeleton because it does not articulate with any other bone. Rather it is suspended from the styloid processes of the temporal bones by ligaments and muscles." That's why it doesn't generally appear on skeletons: There's no bone for it to be wired up to.

Although the hyoid bone is well protected by soft tissue and difficult to break, Roesch points out that, in the event of strangulation, "the hyoid bone and cartilages of the larynx and trachea are often fractured." According to Robert B. Pickering in *The Use of Forensic Anthropology*, this means that, during postmortem examination, should this bone be found to be broken, the cause of death is very likely to be strangulation.

A LOST ADULT TOOTH CAN BE REPLANTED

LOSING A PERMANENT TOOTH DOESN'T HAVE TO BE PERMANENT. A tooth that has been knocked out can be quickly and easily refitted—providing you can find it. In *Harty's Endodontics in Clinical*

Practice, Thomas R. Pitt Ford advises that the tooth "should be replaced as soon as possible, preferably at the site of the accident," ensuring of course that it is refitted the right way around. Donna Phinney and Judy Halstead, writing in *Delmar's Handbook of Essential Skills and Procedures for Chairside Dental Assisting,* qualify this by ex- plaining that knocked-out baby teeth are not suitable for replacement due to the fact that "infection...may occur."

In the *Handbook of Pediatric Dentistry,* Angus C. Cameron and Richard P. Widmer advise that if it is impractical to refit the tooth in situ, "store the tooth in milk or saltwater"; they also suggest that contact-lens solution is ideal. *Harty's* adds that "if the tooth has been dry for more than one hour" the refit is less likely to be successful. Finally, the *Handbook* sensibly instructs the tooth-loser to "seek urgent dental treatment."

PERSPIRATION HAS NO ODOR

AFTER EXCESSIVE SWEAT-PRODUCING EXERTION, WHO HASN'T FELT anxious about the possibility of emitting that horror of horrors: body odor. The good news, we are assured by Megan Tranter in *Occupational Hygiene and Risk Management,* is that sweat, or more politely, perspiration, "is odorless." In *Nursing Care of the Skin,* Rebecca Penzer agrees, explaining that sweat glands "secrete a sticky odorless substance."

As you might have guessed, though, it's not all good news. Penzer adds that "the substance is rapidly acted on by bacteria, thus creating a smell that is most commonly known as body odor." Tranter agrees, and reveals that sweat "can have a musky odor if decomposed by bacteria on the skin." The *Encyclopaedia Britannica* explains why: "Skin bacteria break down the fats into unsaturated fatty acids that possess a pungent odor." So it isn't the sweat itself that offends, but the smell of the resultant fatty acids.

Indeed, fresh perspiration at low concentration can have quite a draw since it contains sex pheromones. James V. Kohl and Robert T. Francoeur's fascinating volume *The Scent of Eros* describes experiments where a synthesized pheromone similar to androstenone in male sweat was sprayed onto an office waiting-room chair and into selected telephone booths. While "men avoided the chair," it appeared that "most women seemed attracted" to it. As for the scented phone booths: "Both men and women spent more time on the phone" in those booths. (According to Kohl and Francoeur, gents, this substance "smells almost exactly like sandal-wood.")

Thus, if you should break out into a sweat, flirt quickly with a handy member of the opposite sex before your short-lived sexual magnetism is broken down into stinky B. O. by those bothersome bacteria.

CAUCASIAN BABIES ARE BORN BLUE-EYED

IT IS THE PIGMENT MELANIN THAT GIVES THE IRIS ITS DISTINCTIVE color, while the color itself is determined by genetics. Brown eyes are generally dominant over blue: Caucasian couples often speculate on what color their baby's eyes will be. Indeed, many proud parents can be heard to announce that their newborn has blue eyes. However, it would be surprising if they said otherwise, because according to A. M. Winchester in *Genetics: A Survey of the*

Principles of Heredity, "nearly all babies of the Caucasian race are born with blue eyes" because eye pigment only develops after the baby is born. Rosalind Stollery in her work *Ophthalmic Nursing* explains that iris color depends on the amount of pigment "laid down in the stroma [membrane covering the eye] after birth." A few days after birth "the baby's eyes become darker... [and] the more melanin laid down, the darker the eyes become."

In *What to Expect* by Murkoff, Eisenberg, and Hathaway, the authors explain that "Caucasian babies are born with dark blue or slate-colored eyes; most dark-skinned infants with dark, usually brown, eyes." They go on to add that "while the dark eyes of the darker-skinned babies will stay dark, the eye color of Caucasian babies may go through a number of changes... before becoming set somewhere between three and six months, or even later." Indeed, "since pigmentation of the iris may continue increasing during the entire first year, the depth of color may not be evident until around baby's first birthday."

As a point of interest, the *Genetics Problem Solver* (Research and Education Association) explains that we have such a wide variety of eye colors thanks to "modifier genes." Blue eyes appear blue due to "the scattering of white light by the almost colorless cells of the outer iris." But surprisingly, it's quite possible for a blue-eyed couple to have brown-eyed offspring. This can happen if one of them carries the brown-eye gene, but has a lack of pigmentation (blue eyes) due to the effect of "modifier genes." In other words, the brown pigment was prevented from developing in the parent's eyes due to the modifier gene, but features in the child due to the child's own genetic mix.

A CAUCASIAN COUPLE CAN HAVE A BIRACIAL BABY

THE FABLED "THROWBACK BABY" IS OFTEN DISMISSED AS PURE MYTH, but although it is a rarity, it can occur. One such case is recounted in the moving story of a South African woman named Sandra Laing. Biographer Judith Stone recounts Sandra's story in *When She Was White*. In 1955, in apartheid South Africa, Sandra was born to white parents. By the time she went to school her skin color and features had taken on a biracial appearance. Her parentage was questioned, and, under the apartheid system, she was obliged to leave her family and transfer to a school for nonwhites. Recessive genes were responsible for Sandra's predicament.

In *Introduction to the Anatomy and Physiology of Children*, Janet MacGregor explains that recessive genes are " 'hidden' by the dominant genes . . . [and] provide the 'throwback' phenomenon produced when both parents carry the recessive characteristic." For Sandra to be born to Caucasian parents, both parents must have had a genetic history containing some black genes. (Conversely, MacGregor explains that such recessive genes could also result in a biracial couple producing a child that has a Caucasian appearance.)

More recently, in March 2006, the *Daily Mail* reported that a biracial woman had given birth to fraternal twin girls, one of Caucasian appearance and one of biracial appearance. Her partner, the father of the twins, is also biracial. The Multiple Births Foundation explained that one baby had "inherited the black genes from both sides of the family" while her sister had "inherited the white ones." It was further explained that skin color is thought to be determined by up to seven different genes working together. Biracial individuals usually have an assortment of genes coding for both black and white skin. Such a couple will normally have a baby who resembles both parents equally. But, very occasionally, the egg or sperm might contain genes coding for one skin color only. If both the egg and sperm contain all white genes, the baby will be white. If both contain only the genetic coding for black skin, the baby will be black.

Some years later, blood tests confirmed that Sandra was the child of her Caucasian parents and she was therefore reclassified as white. However, Sandra, who felt happier and more accepted in the black community, eloped with a black South African at the age of sixteen and had two children. To complicate matters further, the fact that Sandra was now classified as white meant that under apartheid law she was not permitted to live under the same roof as her nonwhite children. Sandra's father was unwilling to allow her to change her racial status for the sake of her children, and so she had to wait until she was twenty-one before she could reclassify herself as nonwhite.

Thanks to the proceeds generated by the telling of her intriguing background, Sandra has now been able to make a life for herself and declares herself "much happier." Her story appears to illustrate that, just like eye color, skin color is a complex genetic lottery unconstrained by borders or beliefs.

CHAPTER 11

Science *and* Nature

MODERN DOG BREEDS WERE GENETICALLY ENGINEERED BY HUMANS

THE ODD AND ARGUABLY COMICAL APPEARANCE OF THE DACHSHUND is not due to natural causes. In *The Dog*, author Linda P. Case points out that "although breeds can differ significantly in appearance and temperament, natural selection is not the cause of their development. Rather, a breed is a direct result of artificial selection by humans." In *The Genetics of the Dog* (edited by Anatoly Ruvinsky and J. Sampson), it is claimed that "the archaeological record suggests that the first domestic dogs were found in the Middle East around 12,000 to 14,000 years ago," while Case adds, "It is estimated that selective breeding of dogs for special functions and appearance has occurred for around 3,000 to 5,000 years." Ruvinsky and Sampson explain that "molecular genetic data consistently support the origin of dogs from wolves," and point out that the very first, ancient dog breeds include "the dingo...the New Guinea singing dog... and the Mexican hairless." The Romans then developed mastiffs and greyhounds.

Indeed, nineteenth-century naturalist Charles Darwin noticed that domesticated dogs, thanks to human intervention, appeared to have evolved unnatural body shapes, ill-suited to life in the wild. The hound/terrier cross that is the dachshund—originally bred to pursue badgers into burrows—would have some difficulty outrunning a hungry wolf, or even a peckish rat. In his 1868 work *The Variation of Animals and Plants Under Domestication* (Volume 1), Darwin notes that "the breeding of dogs" goes back to "ancient times," and comments that a "peculiarity" that could arguably be termed a "monstrosity" may "be increased and fixed by man's selection." In other words, a mutation in a dog, which would normally die out, if it were useful to humans could be deliberately incorporated into the breed by "selective breeding." Case confirms this, explaining that "many of the extreme alterations in form and function of the dog...occurred only within the past 150 to 200 years."

Darwin suggests that certain breeds suffered "evil effects of long-continued close interbreeding." The inbreeding continued unchecked until the twentieth century, and, in recent years, the appearance of the breed has been given greater weight than its "usefulness." For this reason, as veterinarian Dan Rice points out in *The Dog Handbook*, "purebred dogs generally have more genetic faults and deformities than do mixed breeds." For example, many King Charles spaniels suffer with heart problems, a large percentage of Dalmatians are deaf, and many dachshunds are destined to endure spinal problems. Nowadays, responsible dog breeders are well aware of these issues and are actively striving to improve the health of "purebred" dogs.

BONE CHINA CONTAINS BONES

YOU MAY NOT ADMIRE THE OPALESCENCE OF YOUR FINE CHINA IN quite the same light when you learn of Mary Frank Gaston's revelation in the *Collector's Encyclopedia of English China* that "bone paste (or bone china) was so called because its principal ingredient was...an ash made from calcined animal bones." Author of *Ceramic Technology for Potters and Sculptors* Yvonne Hutchinson Cuff agrees: "The material that distinguishes bone china from other ceramic bodies is animal-bone ash."

The process, which results in more durable products than those made from porcelain, began life in the eighteenth century. In *Conservation and Restoration of Ceramics*, Susan Buys and Victoria Oakley explain that English potter Thomas Frye "patented the recipe for a body [clay mixture] that included the addition of a small amount of calcified bone as a flux." They add that about fifty years later, Joseph Spode II modified the mixture so that "half the body consisted of bone ash."

In case you were wondering, the other constituents of bone china are generally china clay and Cornish stone. Now that we have established that bone-china plates contain real bone, perhaps it's worth stocking up on paper plates for vegetarian dinner guests. At least it would save on the dishwashing.

INDIGO WAS ADDED TO THE RAINBOW TO MAKE THE COLORS ADD UP TO "LUCKY" SEVEN

HAVE YOU EVER WONDERED WHY THERE ARE SEVEN COLORS IN THE light spectrum, affectionately known as the rainbow, and only six colors in the artist's color spectrum? In *Understanding Color,*

Linda Holtzschue points out that eighteenth-century German writer, poet, and scholar Johann Wolfgang von Goethe's six-hue spectrum "remains the convention of the artists" whereas "Newton's seven-hue model ... remains the scientist's (physical) spectrum." She theorizes that "because the students who pursue sciences are rarely the same ones who go into the visual arts, the differences between the two ideas ... generally go unnoticed."

The extra color in the light spectrum is indigo, which Holtzschue claims that many people can't distinguish as a separate color. This may be because, as education lecturer Steve Farrow claims in *The Really Useful Science Book*, "There are actually only six colors in the well-known rainbow of light."

Goethe's symmetrical color wheel stands up to scrutiny. Farrow describes how the three primary colors—red, yellow, and blue—mix in pairs to form the three secondary colors—orange, green, and purple—and "these six colors are present in the rainbow." So how did blue become blue *and* indigo in the light spectrum?

Seventeenth-century English physicist and mathematician Sir Isaac Newton split sunlight through a prism and named the resulting colors. "It is tempting," writes Farrow, "to imagine that the great man 'saw' seven colors in his rainbow." But since Newton was also an alchemist, "seven was a lucky number." Holtzschue agrees: "Mysticism was a great part of Newton's time." She theorizes that "he may have elected to include seven colors because of mystical properties associated with the number seven."

Nineteenth-Century Theories of Art (edited by Joshua C. Taylor) explains that "Newton saw seven colors in the prism, doubtless to find a poetical analogy with the seven notes of music; he has arbitrarily introduced, under the name of *indigo*, a seventh color which is only a shade of *blue*... it is a licence that even the greatness of his genius cannot excuse."

In *Introduction to Light*, author Gary Waldman explains that "more commonly today we only speak of six major divisions, leaving out indigo... [because] a careful reading of Newton's work indicates that the color he called indigo, we would normally call blue: His blue is then what we would name blue-green or cyan." Waldman reveals that Newton derived the term "spectra" for the colors he saw, from the word "spectre" meaning "ghost." The collection of colors he termed "a spectrum."

Of course, color-naming is subjective, and technically speaking every hue has its place in the spectrum. But if you find that you can't make out the sixth color in the rainbow, don't worry, you're not alone.

ALGAE ARE THE LUNGS OF THE WORLD

OXYGEN IS VITAL TO LIFE: WE BREATHE IT IN AND CONVERT IT TO energy to maintain our very existence. But where does all the oxygen come from? *Intimate Strangers: Unseen Life on Earth* (Cynthia Needham and colleagues) explains that oxygen "is the principal waste product of photosynthesis." It goes on to suggest that "as much as half the total oxygen that we breathe" is contributed by algae. Most people think only of plants when it comes to this process, and therefore "the contribution of photosynthetic microbes may come as a surprise." The *Encyclopaedia Britannica* goes further, claiming that "the waters of the world are the main oxygen generators of the biosphere; their algae are estimated to replace about 90 percent of all oxygen used."

In *Trouble in Paradise*, sociology professor J. Timmons Roberts and Nikki Demetria Thanos reveal that "the algae are the real lungs of the world," and they describe how "90 percent of the world's oxygen is produced by underwater algae called phytoplankton."

Consequently, *Human Biology and Health: An Evolutionary Approach* (edited by Davey, Halliday, and Hirst) reveals that phytoplankton are "a critical source of significant amounts of oxygen in the atmosphere" and that because of this "a significant reduction in phytoplankton will ultimately lead to global loss of animal and plant biodiversity."

THE MOON CONTROLS THE TIDES

THERE ARE MANY ANCIENT MYTHS AND SUPERSTITIONS RELATING TO the moon. These beliefs date back centuries and exist all over the world. The moon was believed to foretell disaster and induce madness. Indeed the word "lunatic" stems from "lunar," from the Latin *luna*, meaning "the moon." Ancient Greek philosopher Aristotle believed the position of the sun and the phases of the moon related to the tides. Although it sounds like archaic superstition, modern science has found the belief to be correct.

It's a very complicated relationship, but in *A Student's Guide to the Seashore* by John and Susan Fish, it is revealed that "tides result from the gravitational forces between the moon and the sun." Dennis Graver, author of *Scuba Diving*, explains further that the earth "pulls water toward the moon," and the resulting increase in water depth is known as a "high tide." Water pulled away from the sides of the earth produces a decrease in water depth called "low tide." Here is a little more detail from *Scuba Diving* to help clarify matters: A high tide forms on the side of the earth opposite the moon because "the attraction of the moon is least at that point and because of the centrifugal effect created by the rotation of the earth." At any given time, "two areas on the earth are experiencing high tides and two areas are experiencing low tides."

The mysterious names given to tides have always intrigued me, so here is a brief rundown courtesy of Dr. David A. Ross, writing in *The Fishermen's Ocean.* The combined gravitational pull of the sun and the moon causes a "spring tide," which is relatively strong. The name comes not from the time of year, but because it is said to " 'spring forth' onto the coast." Spring tides occur around once a fortnight (every two weeks), at about the time of the new moon and full moon.

When the sun and the moon "work against each other" this produces a "neap (inactive) tide," which is, as the name implies, much weaker. These also occur once a fortnight—"at first-quarter moon and last- or third-quarter moon."

We no longer believe that the moon warns of disaster or sends us mad, but there still remains much to learn about this celestial satellite.

NATURAL GAS HAS NO ODOR

THE HIGHLY FLAMMABLE SUBSTANCE KNOWN AS natural gas is made up mainly of methane and ethane, and is a type of petroleum that occurs naturally deep in the ground, generally along with crude oil. It was discovered in England in 1659 and its use has become widespread across Europe. The reassuringly titled *Natural Gas in Nontechnical Language*, edited by Rebecca L. Busby, states that "in 1821 in Fredonia, New York, a gunsmith, William Hart, drilled America's first natural gas well." The gas was prevented from escaping by means of "a large barrel." According to Busby's book, this new innovation of natural gas "was used to light the town's streets in honor of [American Revolutionary hero] General Lafayette's visit."

Prior to the use of natural gas, Europe and America relied on "manufactured" gas, which was made, as Busby's book explains, by "heating coal." This "coal gas" was known as "town gas" and was used for lighting.

As anyone who accidentally leaves the gas unlit knows, the resulting smell is most unpleasant. However, in *Gas Installation Technology*, Roy D. Treloar reveals that "natural gas...is odorless." The *Encyclopaedia Britannica* agrees that "the principal ingredient of gas is methane, which is...odorless." Busby's work also describes it as "a colorless, odorless gas that burns readily with a pale, slightly luminous flame."

Treloar goes on to explain that "odorants, such as diethyle sulphide and ethyl butyle mereaptan, are added at the point of distribution to give the gas a recognizable smell." Busby's book confirms that "the characteristic odor of natural gas is added artificially." The volume goes on to explain that "odor is a very important step in the distribution process and is required by federal safety regulations." Indeed, "if the pipeline gas is received with insufficient odor, it must be odorized before leaving the city gate station."

The odorant confers a "gassy" smell that makes the presence of escaping and unburned gas recognizable at very low concentrations. Busby explains that "this warns customers well before the gas can accumulate to hazardous levels." According to Busby's book, "mixtures of air and natural gas are explosive over the range of 5 percent to 15 percent natural gas." To ensure safety, odorized gas is detectable "at a concentration of just 1 percent." Natural gas smells unpleasant because it's designed that way: Better to experience a brief noxious odor than to inadvertently blow oneself up a few hours later....

THE TROPICAL BUTTERFLY PEA PLANT IS NAMED AFTER THE CLITORIS

IN EIGHTEENTH-CENTURY TROPICAL Asia, Swedish botanist Carl Linnaeus discovered a fetching new plant that many know by its common name, the butterfly pea. With a delicate lavender-mauve flower, this pretty plant is not as showy as a sweet pea, but it does have a familiar look to it—similar to that cottage-garden perennial, the everlasting pea. Linnaeus must have thought it looked familiar to him too, since, as Nico Vermeulen notes in *Encyclopaedia of House Plants*, Linnaeus named the plant *Clitoria ternatea* because he "thought this flower looked like a clitoris." (*Ternate* means "triple-leafed" in Latin.)

Robert Geneve, writing in *A Book of Blue Flowers*, describes the flower thus: "*Clitoria* is a group of mostly tropical herbaceous and woody perennials. The flowers are somewhat pealike and tucked among the foliage." Geneve adds that "the genus name refers to the resemblance of the flower to a clitoris." Indeed, in Linnaeus's *Philosophia Botanica*, written in 1775, next to "*Clitoria,*" the renowened doctor and botanist noted that the flower is so called "from the shape of the corolla (clitoris)."

Other genitally inspired plant names include the orchid and the avocado. *Orkhis* is Greek for "testicle" (the bulbous root was thought to resemble the organ), and "avocado" derives from the Aztec word for testicle, *ahuacatl*. The foul-smelling stinkhorn mushroom's Latin name, *Phallus impudicus*, means "shameless penis," and if you've ever seen one, you'll understand why. Conversely, the passion flower was named not because its showy flowers were considered erotic, but because a seventeenth-century monk thought that the flower parts seemed symbolic of different aspects of the "Passion" (suffering) of Christ.

Orchids, stinkhorns, and passion flowers are relatively common plants, but as Vermeulen laments, although *Clitoria ternatea* is well worth the hunt, this "beautiful climber" can be very difficult to find.

CHAPTER 12

Names *and* Their Histories

SCOTCH TAPE WAS NAMED AFTER THE SUPPOSED STINGINESS OF ITS INVENTOR'S BOSSES

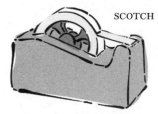

SCOTCH TAPE, INVENTED BY RICHARD G. DREW, was the first ever adhesive tape. He created it in 1925 while employed by the Minnesota Mining and Manufacturing Company. (The founders and employees referred to the company as "3M Company," which is how it officially became known in 2002.)

A Century of Innovation, 3M's centenary publication, features the story of how Drew invented a tape to help 1920s automobile painters achieve a better finish on cars with "the popular, two-tone style...Either the paint came off when painters tried to remove the plaster tape they used, or the tape's adhesive—softened by lacquer solvent—remained on the car's surface."

Virginia Huck, author of *Brand of the Tartan: The 3M Story*, which chronicled the first fifty years of the company, explains that when Drew's revolutionary new masking tape was first marketed, the company, "as an economy measure," applied adhesive only to the "outer edges of the two-inch strips, leaving the center plain." One edge was to be taped to masking paper; the other was to be taped to the car to hold the paper in place. According to Huck, "3M's stinginess with the glue turned out to be a new headache to car painters." The partially coated tape didn't stick well and the story is that these painters growled at 3M salesmen, "Why be so Scotch with the adhesive?"

As 3M explains on the company website, "the tape improved, but the name stuck" and was officially trademarked Scotch Brand.

MICHELANGELO AND REMBRANDT WERE THE RESPECTIVE ARTISTS' FIRST NAMES

THREE GREAT ITALIANS, THIRTEENTH-CENTURY POET DANTE, fourteenth-century physicist Galileo, and sixteenth-century artist Michelangelo all have something—besides their genius—in common: They are all known by their first names. Galileo was Galileo Galilei, Dante's full name was Durante Alighieri, and Michelangelo's family name was di Lodovico Buonarroti Simoni. In *Remarkable Physicists*, Ioan James explains that any great Italian of that period was "universally known by his first name rather than by his family name."

The same held true, in later centuries, in other parts of Europe. Seventeenth-century Dutch painter Rembrandt's full name was Rembrandt Harmenszoon van Rijn, and fellow nineteenth-century Dutchman van Gogh signed himself Vincent. Both Rembrandt and van Gogh began with longer signatures, then shortened them to their given names. Was this done out of self-importance, with the implication that they were so famous they didn't need to include a family name? Probably not. Van Gogh gives an insight into why he took to signing himself Vincent in a letter to his brother: "I sign so that those who see me understand that I am saying 'thou' to them." In other words, he was saying to anyone who gazes upon his works—I bare my soul to you as if you are my close friend.

Nowadays, we are still on first-name terms with the famous. Italian-American performer Madonna Ciccone is known by her first name alone. It helps, of course if that name is unusual. In *Madonna "Talking"* by Mick St. Michael she is quoted as saying, "My mother is the only other person I have heard of named Madonna."

THE *S* IN HARRY S. TRUMAN
DOESN'T STAND FOR ANYTHING

THE THIRTY-THIRD PRESIDENT OF THE UNITED STATES, HARRY S. Truman, doesn't have a middle name, just a middle initial. In her biographical work *Harry S. Truman,* Deborah Cannarella explains that baby Truman's first name came from his uncle Harrison Young, "but his parents could not agree on the boy's middle name." Harry's father favored Shippe, after his own father, but Cannarella reveals that "Harry's mother ... wanted to name him Solomon after her father." The Trumans struck a compromise and named Harry "after both grandfathers." Harry's middle initial *S* therefore stood for Solomon *and* Shippe. *The Cambridge Encyclopedia of the English Language* confirms this with a quote from Truman's daughter Margaret: "To placate their touchy elders, his parents added an *S.,* but studiously refrained from deciding whether it stood for Solomon or Shippe."

Since the *S* doesn't stand for anything, it is sometimes argued by those with pedantic natures that, strictly speaking, there should be no period after it. Indeed, Truman once joked about this very point. However, most examples of Truman's signature show the period clearly in situ, and *The Christian Writer's Manual of Style* also assures us that "Truman himself put a period after it." He must surely be the final arbiter on his own name.

Another Harry who had a middle initial but no middle name is the late British actor Harry H. Corbett. He adopted the initial to distinguish himself from Harry Corbett the puppeteer, and joked that the *H* stood for "hanything."

THE NAME "WENDY" FIRST APPEARED IN J. M. BARRIE'S PLAY *PETER PAN*

MANY FORENAMES HAVE ANCIENT HISTORIES. SOME originate from surnames and others evoke prized objects, but "Wendy" is a little different. It evolved from "friendy-wendy," a diminutive of "friend," and found its way into Scottish dramatist J. M. Barrie's 1904 children's play *Peter Pan*, through Barrie's friendship with Margaret, the small daughter of poet W. E. Henley.

In his biographical work *J. M. Barrie and the Lost Boys*, Andrew Birkin explains that the diminutive Margaret referred to Barrie as her "Friendy," but since she couldn't pronounce the letter *r* it came out as "Wendy." *Names New and Old* (volume edited by E. Wallace McMullen) gives a slight variation of the derivation, explaining that Margaret called Barrie " 'Friendly,' which became 'Friendy-Wendy,' then 'Wendy.' "

Sadly, Margaret Henley died at the age of six, but clearly she made such a strong impression on Barrie that he incorporated her nickname for him into what has become one of the most popular children's plays of all time.

THE CANARY ISLANDS ARE NAMED AFTER DOGS

THIS ARCHIPELAGO OF ISLANDS IN THE ATLANTIC OCEAN IS, NOWAdays, a popular vacation destination, but it was less hospitable to the Romans in the first century B.C., according to Pliny the Elder, who passed on the findings of King Juba II of Mauritius, who had sent an expedition there. The island of "Canaria [is] so called from the multitude of dogs [*canes*] of great size." In *The World of Juba II and Kleopatra Selene*, Duane W. Roller reveals that when the explorers returned they presented their king with two of these huge dogs. (Doubtless he would have much preferred a straw donkey.)

"Canary" derives from the Latin for "dog," *canis*, from which we get the word "canine." The connection with dogs is also linked to the North African tribe the Canarii, who, according to Pliny, were so named because "they partake of their food in common with the canine race, and share with it the entrails of wild beasts."

Canary birds do come from the Canary Islands, but, as explained in *Beautiful Birds* by Alvin and Virginia Silverstein, "Canaries were named after the Canary Islands" and not the other way round. The Canary dog (*Presa Canario*), which originated in the islands, conjures up a comical image of a hound/canary cross, but, in reality, it's a huge, fierce beast, not well disposed to strangers. How King Juba must have rejoiced at his two hulking canine gifts.

It's just as well the Canary Islands kept their

Latin name: As vacation destinations go, the "Isle of Dogs" doesn't have quite the same allure.

MARLBORO CIGARETTES GOT THEIR NAME FROM A LONDON STREET

MARLBORO CIGARETTES ARE UNMISTAKABLY AMERICAN, YET THEIR origins lie elsewhere. In *The London Companion*, edited by Jo Swinnerton, we learn that "the all-American Marlboro brand of cigarettes was named after the Philip Morris factory, which in 1902 was situated on Marlborough Street." Great Marlborough Street, London, dates back to 1704, and was named in honor of John Churchill, 1st Duke of Marlborough.

Mollenkamp, Levy, Menn, and Rothfeder, writing in *The People vs. Big Tobacco*, give a little more detail: In 1847, British tobacconist Philip Morris opened a London tobacco store that sold pipes, cigars, and cigarettes. A few years later, Morris started up his own Philip Morris cigarette label, which was eventually taken over by British industrialist William Thomson. Thomson "exported Philip Morris cigarettes to the United States." In *The Tobacco Book*, Dr. David B. Moyer reveals that originally the Marlboro cigarette was "intro-duced in 1924 as a woman's cigarette." These were called "Marlboro Beauty Tips and had their end colored red 'to conceal those telltale lipstick traces.'" The volume adds that the cigarette "was advertised with the slogan 'Mild as May.'"

Sales took off in the U.S., and by 1940 the Philip Morris Company was in fourth position with "a 10 percent market share" for the cigarette which had, by this time, taken on the American spelling of "Marlboro."

OPRAH WINFREY GAINED HER FIRST NAME DUE TO A SPELLING MIX-UP

TALK-SHOW HOST AND ACTRESS OPRAH WINFREY HAS AN UNUSUAL, not to say unique, first name. While speaking in a 1999 *Academy of Achievement* interview, Oprah stated that she was born in rural Mississippi in 1954. When speaking of how she came by her first name, Oprah explained that "my name had been chosen from the Bible" by her aunt Ida. However, there is no "Oprah" in the Bible. This is because the name Aunt Ida chose from The Book of Ruth was, in fact, "Orpah."

Many biblical names have meanings. For example, the *Dictionary of Patron Saints' Names*, compiled by Thomas W. Sheehan, gives the meaning of the Hebrew name Ruth as "compassionate, beautiful friend." However, the meaning of the name Orpah, according to Robert L. Hubbard writing in *The Book of Ruth*, "remains an unsolved mystery." The work adds that possible derivations could be from the Hebrew *orep*, which means "back of the neck," *ugar*, which means "clouds," or possibly the Arabic *gurfa*, which means "handful of water."

Oprah's name, as she explains, "went down as 'Orpah' on my birth certificate," but Oprah did not get the chance to be addressed by the established biblical name because "people didn't know how to pronounce it." The upshot was that "they put the *P* before the *R*." In *Oprah Winfrey*, biographer Katherine E. Krohn confirms that "nobody seemed to know how to spell Orpah, the biblical name the family had chosen from The Book of Ruth."

It is sometimes maintained that Oprah's name was misspelled on her birth certificate, but Oprah confirms that "on the birth certificate it is Orpah, but then it got translated to Oprah." Krohn agrees that "in spite of the fact that the official document reads 'Orpah,' that name isn't used anywhere else, so the spelling became the one we know today."

Oprah seems perfectly happy with her name, having commented that "Oprah spells Harpo backwards. I don't know what Orpah spells...."

CHAPTER 13

World History

PASSAGES CONDEMNING SLAVERY WERE CUT FROM THOMAS JEFFERSON'S 1776 DECLARATION OF INDEPENDENCE

IN 1776, AFTER THE OUTBREAK OF THE REVOLUTIONARY WAR, THE Second Continental Congress convened and charged Thomas Jefferson with the task of drafting the Declaration of

Independence. A copy is included in *The Papers of Thomas Jefferson* (Volume I) transcribed by Professor Julian P. Boyd.

Jefferson began his declaration with the words "We hold these truths to be sacred & undeniable; that all men are created equal," yet slavery wasn't abolished in America until 1865. It would appear that the near-century delay in making good the "sacred & undeniable truth" was most likely due to Jefferson's slave trade condemnation having been edited out of the final draft. The *Encyclopaedia Britannica* reveals that the American Congress made "substantial changes" to the final draft, and deleted "a denunciation of the African slave trade" because it would have been deemed "offensive to some southern and New England delegates." *Britannica* adds that a reference to "Scotch & foreign mercenaries" was also cut to avoid offending Scotsmen in Congress.

After his opening words, Jefferson's original draft continued: "From that equal creation they derive rights inherent & inalienable, among which are the preservation of life, & liberty, & the pursuit of happiness." This phrase was altered to "that they are endowed by their Creator with certain unalienable Rights," which is decidedly more ambiguous. ("Inalienable" was corrected to "unalienable"; *The Oxford English Dictionary* describes them as synonymous.)

What *Britannica* describes as Jefferson's "denunciation of the African slave trade" passage was a heartfelt diatribe blaming the villain of the day—"his present Majesty" George III—for, as Jefferson complains, "violating . . . [nature's] most sacred rights of life & liberty in the persons of a distant people who never offended him, captivating & carrying them into slavery in another hemisphere, or to incur miserable death in their transportation thither," and being "determined to keep open a market where MEN should be bought & sold."

In *Rebels and Renegades*, professor of American history Neil A. Hamilton explains that Congress reworked and deleted entire passages from Jefferson's original draft for two reasons: firstly because "delegates from South Carolina and Georgia complained about it, supported by northern states that participated in the [slave] trade," but also because "the delegates recognized the contradiction between continuing slavery and fighting for liberty and wanted to avoid calling attention to their enslavement of fellow human beings."

Jefferson freed his own large retinue of slaves (six hundred) upon his death in 1826. While he was alive, he treated his slaves as "my family." (Possibly a little too much like his family, since *Britannica* also reveals that one of his slaves, Sally Hemings, bore several biracial children under his roof, and DNA tests later revealed that "Jefferson was almost certainly the father" of some of them.)

IN CASE OF ATOMIC BOMB ATTACK, THE U.S. GOVERNMENT ADVISED 1950S CITIZENS TO "WEAR A HAT"

IN 1950, AN OFFICIAL U.S. GOVERNMENT booklet entitled *Survival Under Atomic Attack* was circulated. The following year, a public information film of the same name was released, narrated by Edward R. Murrow. The Civil Defense Agency of the Commonwealth of Massachusetts also published its own jaunty five-page pamphlet entitled *Protection from the Atomic Bomb*.

The government booklet states that "while an atom bomb holds more death and destruction than man has ever before wrapped in a single package, its total power is definitely limited." With reference to Hiroshima and Nagasaki, Murrow confides (during footage of a kimono-clad Japanese mother serving bread and butter to three small children) that "the majority of people exposed to radiation recovered completely." He warns against fleeing from an atom bomb, since "an enemy would like nothing better than to have us leave our cities empty and unproductive." The booklet also states that "if you lose your head and blindly attempt to run from the dangers, you may...put tremendous obstacles in the way of your Civil Defense Corps." The Massachusetts pamphlet also advises: "Don't run: there isn't time...crawl under or behind something" and "stay down for at least a minute." A help-

ful illustration shows a citizen jettisoning her handbag and dropping to the ground. This precaution is designed "to let the worst of it pass over you"—apparently. Murrow then reveals the bizarre opinion that "if the people of Hiroshima and Nagasaki had known what we know about civil defense, thousands of lives would have been saved."

The government publication warns against the temptation of looking up "to see what is coming," because it states that the scorching heat can "badly burn the bare skin at two miles." Fortunately, the guide assures readers, "clothing gives protection"; citizens should "always wear full-length, loose-fitting, light-colored" garments, "always wear a hat—the brim may save you a serious face burn," and "never go around with your sleeves rolled up." Who would have thought that ordinary materials like cotton and wool contained such anti-atomic properties?

The Massachusetts guide sagely warns that "too much [radiation] can cause death." It also adds that although "radiation danger is over in a minute," it could "linger for hours." The U.S. booklet advises that civilians "keep all windows and doors closed for at least several hours," and further suggests that they had "better leave them shut until Civil Defense authorities pass the word that there is no lingering radioactivity in your neighborhood," just to be on the safe side.

The state pamphlet recommends that citizens "look for a chance to help others"—such as those poor unfortunates who have tripped over countless discarded handbags, perhaps. But if, as the booklet warns, you do "soak up a serious dose of explosive radioactivity... you most likely would get sick at your stomach and begin to vomit," though equally "you might be sick at your stomach for other reasons, too." (For example, that out-of-date yogurt you recklessly chanced the night before.) The government guidelines further explain that "for a few days you might...feel below par, and about two weeks later most of your hair might fall out." Of course, this unfortunate side effect might be caused by radiation sickness or may simply be brought on by anxiety over where you left your handbag....

AZTECS RIPPED OUT THE HEARTS OF LIVE SACRIFICIAL VICTIMS

SIXTEENTH-CENTURY JESUIT MISSIONARY JOSÉ DE ACOSTA, RESIDENT in Peru and Mexico, recorded how the "Mexicans...labored to take their enemies alive" in order to sacrifice them to their "idols." De Acosta, who witnessed numerous proceedings, reveals in *The Naturall and Morall Historie of the Indies* that "the ordinary manner of sacrificing was to open the stomake...and having pulled out his heart halfe alive, they tumbled the man downe the staires of the Temple." The temple stairs, not surprisingly, were "all imbrewed and defiled with bloud." De Acosta recounts that there were "fortie or fiftie at the least thus sacrificed." One would hope it would end there, but De Acosta goes on to explain that after the unfortunates were slain "their Masters...did eate them, celebrating their Feast and Solemnitie."

Another sixteenth-century source, Franciscan missionary Bernardino de Sahagún, author of *The Florentine Codex: or, The General History of the Things of New Spain,* wrote this account based on eyewitness reports from Aztecs: "And when he [the priest] had laid him [the captive] upon it [the sacrificial stone on the pyramid's temple], the four men stretched him out, [grasping] his arms and legs. And already in the hands of the fire priest laid the [sacrificial knife] ... and then, when he had split open the breast, he at once seized his heart. And he whose breast he laid open was quite alive. And when [the priest] had seized his heart, he dedicated it to the sun."

Anthropology professor Michael E. Smith, writing in *The Aztecs*, puts forward a couple of theories about what prompted such barbaric behavior. "Most Aztecs were deeply religious people ... priests practised sacrifice, and people put up with sacrifice because they believed it was necessary for the continued existence of the universe." In other words, they dared not be the ones to stop the ancient prac-

tice, just in case it angered the gods. A bit like having to make contact with a wooden table every time you use the phrase "touch wood"— only much more gory.

Alternatively, Smith suggests that the sacrifices may have been a means to demonstrate "the awesome power of the gods and the state" to other kingdoms, which would also explain their frequency.

Such horrific practices are, of course, very much frowned upon in modern-day Mexico, and today any tourists are almost entirely guaranteed safety from cannibalism.

ROMANS, WHEN IN BRITAIN,
WORE SOCKS AND UNDERPANTS

IN FILMS, FEARLESS ROMAN SOLDIERS ARE GENER-
ally depicted sockless, and the implication is
that they certainly aren't wearing underpants.
However, we now know differently thanks to correspondence discovered on a wooden tablet at a
Roman auxiliary fort, Vindolanda, at Hadrian's Wall
near the Scottish border. History lecturer and author
of *Roman Britain* David Shotter points out that
"these tablets revealed people with surprisingly
modern preoccupations—acquiring socks and underpants." The
wooden "letter" in question was sent from an unknown corre-
spondent to a soldier and stated, "I have sent you ... pairs of socks
(*undorum*) from Sattua [possibly a place name or a person], two
pairs of sandals (*solearum duo*) and two pairs of underpants (*subli-
gariorum duo*)." Alan K. Bowman, author of *Roman Frontier*, confirms this unlikely-sounding scenario: "As for clothing, the very
first tablet to be discovered at Vindolanda vividly illustrates the
casual despatch of such items at a level probably lower than the
officer class: the writer records the dispatch of twenty pairs of
socks, two pairs of sandals and two pairs of underpants."

Thus far, no artifacts have been found that record the wearing
of underpants by Romans stationed in southern Britain. Possibly,
the necessity for them only arose when the Mediterranean fighting force ventured into the chilly northern regions.

Very few Roman undies have come to light during excavations. Writing in *Roman Records from Vindolanda and Hadrian's
Wall*, director of the Vindolanda Trust Robert Birley explains
that excavations have unearthed various footwear, such as sandals

and boots, but so far "only one small sock." He adds that "underpants have yet to be located."

Since only two pairs appear to have been sent at a time, they probably saw quite a bit of service. Perhaps it's best that Roman underpants, should they still exist, remain undiscovered.

PIRATES FORCED VICTIMS TO WALK THE PLANK

THIS SEAFARING PRACTICE FEATURES IN CLASSIC CHILDREN'S LITERAture such as J. M. Barrie's *Peter Pan* as well as modern-day films, including *Pirates of the Caribbean*. David Cordingly, curator at the National Maritime Museum and author of *Under the Black Flag*, points out that since no seventeenth- and eighteenth-century written accounts of walking the plank exist, most writers on piracy have "dismissed the practice as a myth created and made popular by works of fiction."

However, first-century Greek historian Plutarch, writing in his *Life of Julius Caesar*, regales us with a fascinating story about a juvenile Julius Caesar being captured by Cilician pirates and unwittingly prompting the plank-walking practice. According to Plutarch, eighteen-year-old Julius Caesar "was taken near the island Pharmacusa by ... pirates, who, at that time, with large fleets of ships and innumerable smaller vessels infested the seas everywhere." While on board one of their ships Caesar managed to aggravate the pirates on two counts: Firstly, he insisted on their raising his ransom of twenty talents to fifty, and then he lorded it over them despite the fact that he was *their* captive. However, the ransom was paid and Caesar was set free.

Armed to the teeth, Caesar promptly returned to the pirates, who were, some might argue, foolishly "still stationed at the island," and captured them. While the Governor of Asia was pondering the punishment, Caesar "ordered the pirates to be brought forward and crucified."

According to Don C. Seitz, writing in his work also named *Under the Black Flag*, after this incident pirates would always "bow low and tender their most humble services" to all Roman captives, then politely request their victim "to mount upon the ship's ladder and step to liberty—into the sea!"

No early accounts of plank-walking exist, but nineteenth-century journalist Hezekiah Niles records in his *Weekly Register* that in 1822 pirates captured the Jamaican sloop *Blessing*, and since the ill-fated Captain William Smith was unable to furnish them with coinage (he only had flour and cornmeal) "a plank was run out in the starboard side of the vessel, upon which he [the pirate chief] made Captain Smith walk." When the unfortunate captain got to the end "they tilted the plank, then he dropped into the sea." Captain Smith attempted to swim, but the heartless pirate chief "fired at him therewith, when he sank, and was seen no more."

Captain Smith was fortunate in being able to swim (not that it did him much good), but others, when faced with the same punishment, would be let down by their lack of swimming skills. The nineteenth-century journal *Macmillan's Magazine* includes a tale in which a character reveals, "Many of our English sailors cannot swim." He continues, "Many gentlemen in various professions, to whom that accomplishment would be not only useful, but perhaps absolutely necessary, are equally ignorant of it."

The Times of 1829 carried another report of enforced plank-walking. The Dutch brig *Vhan Fredericka* was looted by a band of thirty pirates, and when the Dutchmen made protest—as one would—they were "laughed at by the ruffians, who proceeded deliberately to compel the wretched men to what is termed 'walk the plank.'" One passenger escaped to tell the tale by revealing "the whereabouts of…gold" and was later put ashore on Cuba.

Do no early accounts of walking the plank exist because witnesses of the practice were very likely also dispatched by this method? In truth, walking the plank was a rarity. Cordingly explains that most pirate victims were unceremoniously thrown over the side, since this method of dispatch was much less time-consuming.

MANHATTAN WAS PURCHASED FOR SIXTY GUILDERS

"I'LL TAKE MANHATTAN, the Bronx, and Staten Island too." The words of the hit song from the 1920s show *Garrick Gaieties* take on a whole new meaning when applied to seventeenth-century Belgian Walloon Peter Minuit.

In 1624, Dutch merchants arrived in the New World to found a settlement that became known as New Netherland. Minuit settled along with them, becoming director-general. The nineteenth-century New York judge Murray Hoffman, writing in his 1862 work *Treatise Upon the Estate and Rights of the Corporation of the City of New York, as Proprietors*, explained that Minuit, on behalf of the West Indian Company, "purchased from the Indians, who were the indubitable owners thereof, the Island of the Manhattes, situated at the entrance of the…river." Hoffman goes on to reveal that Minuit "then laid the foundation of a city."

The *Oxford Concise Dictionary of World Place-Names* by John Everett-Heath states that the island of Manhattan was "named after a Native American tribe, the Manhattan." Hoffman adds that the purchase was announced in a letter from Peter Schagen to the States General dated November 5, 1626. The letter explains that Minuit had "purchased the island Manhattes from the Indians, for the value of sixty guilders [a Dutch coin]" and goes on to point out that the area was "eleven thousand morgens [a Dutch unit of measurement of land equivalent to about two acres] in size." The letter continues: "They had all their grain sowed by the middle of May, and reaped by the middle of August."

The *Encyclopaedia Britannica* suggests that the tribe who sold the land was "the Manhattan, a tribe of the Wappinger Confederacy." Everett-Heath agrees that the Manhattan tribe "sold it [the island] to Peter Minuit...in 1626" although *The New Oxford American Dictionary*, edited by Erin McKean, suggests that Minuit "purchased Manhattan Island from the Algonquin Indians." In the letter, there is no mention of how the payment was made, but *Britannica* suggests that it was comprised of "trinkets and cloth valued at sixty guilders, then worth about 1.5 pounds of silver." However, *Britannica* also reveals that in the early seventeenth century, wampum—strings of ceremonial shell beads—were "used as money in trade between whites and Indians because of a shortage of European currency."

Possibly future historians assumed that the debt had been paid in wampum, i.e., beads. This transaction was thought by Minuit to legitimize Dutch colonization of the island. Presumably, the resident Native Americans took the attitude that the settlers could set up camp if they liked and if they were also paying for the privilege, all to the good. Besides, some scholars argue that the tribe Minuit did the deal with was, in reality, the Canarsie, and since they were not resident on the island but merely passing through, whether they were paid in solid silver coinage or wampum or both, they would have made themselves quite a good deal.

TIME WAS DECIMALIZED IN EIGHTEENTH-CENTURY FRANCE

WE TAKE THE MEASUREMENT OF TIME for granted: sixty seconds make a minute, sixty minutes comprise an hour, and so on. Yet, toward the end of the eighteenth century, at the dawn of the French Republic, dates and time were decimalized along with weights and measures.

"Decimal" comes from the Latin *decimus*, meaning "tenth." As explained in *Foundations of Engineering* by Mark T. Holtzapple and Dan Reece, this decimal system was adopted after the French Revolution in an attempt to sever all ties with the traditional Gregorian calendar. The new French Republican calendar still consisted of twelve months but, as the *Encyclopaedia Britannica* explains, they were given seasonal names. For example, January 20 to February 18 was called *Pluviôse*, meaning "rainy." Each month had thirty days (with the leftover five days devoted to festivities), and instead of seven-day weeks, the "month" was divided into three ten-day weeks. Each day had a number and a name. Hervé de Broc, writing in 1891 in *La France Pendant la Révolution*, lists the first three days of *Pluviôse* as *Lauréole* (spurge laurel), *Mousse* (moss), and *Fragon* (butcher's broom).

Then time was decimalized. A 1793 Republican decree stated that "the day, from midnight to midnight, is divided into ten parts: each part into ten others, and so forth down to the smallest measurable time portion." Decimal time required decimal clocks with ten numerals instead of twelve. Holtzapple and Reece explain that the new time period equated to 2.4 hours. Midnight was at ten o'clock and midday was at five o'clock. Each unit was further divided into "millidays" spanning 86.4 seconds.

The Fitzwilliam Museum in Cambridge has a fine example of a decimal mantel clock from this period. The handsome timepiece is equipped with an extra small, twenty-four-hour dial, designed to help French citizens who were struggling with the new decimal system to work out what the time was. The 1793 decree stated that "professors and parents" were required to explain the new decimal system to "the children of the Republic."

The professors and parents of the Republic accepted decimal weights and measures, but declined to accept governmental interference with their time periods, with the result that decimal time was quickly abandoned. Around ten years later, the Republican calendar was also jettisoned.

CHAPTER 14

Biblical Matters

A SEVENTEENTH-CENTURY BIBLE INSTRUCTED READERS TO COMMIT ADULTERY

THE KING JAMES BIBLE, FIRST PUBLISHED IN 1611, DID MUCH TO standardize the varying biblical texts that had gone before. However, the 1631 version, printed in London by the previously reputable publishers Barker and Lucas, was less favorably viewed. *The Wordsworth Dictionary of Phrase and Fable* reveals that "the word 'not' is omitted in the seventh commandment," making the commandment read, "Thou shalt commit adultery." In *A History of the Bible in English*, F. F. Bruce points out that, not surprisingly, Barker and Lucas paid dearly for what became known as the "Wicked Bible," and were fined £300 by Archbishop Laud, which was a fortune in the seventeenth century.

Nor was the 1631 Wicked Bible an isolated case. *The Wordsworth Dictionary of Phrase and Fable* describes a Bible of 1653 printed in Cambridge that was also missing a vital "not," rendering the offending passage as "Know ye not that the unrighteous shall inherit the kingdom of God?"

In a similar vein, the same source quotes J. H. Blunt, writing in *The Anointed Book of Common Prayer* about a correction which, in his opinion, did not need correcting. Blunt complains that the Marriage Service words "till death us depart" (which was perfectly sound English for "divide") was needlessly altered to "till death us do part" in 1661 by the Puritans, "who knew as little of the history of their national language as they did of that of their national church."

The "Treacle Bible" of 1568 inquires: "Is there no tryacle in Gilead?" In fact, the correct word should have been "balm" instead of "tryacle." James A. Duke, author of *Handbook of Nuts*, ex-

plains that the "balm" of the biblical verse was thought to be an oily gum made from the Balanites fruit. He also reveals that "the Douai Bible of 1609 translates the passage as 'Is there no rosin in Gilead?'" Presumably, when translating the word for the oily gum substance, treacle was felt to be a more accurate Western equivalent than the more traditional choice of balm: a case of biblical translators being a little *too* pedantic, perhaps.

A not-so-good book known as the Irish Bible of 1716 advises the devout to "sin on more" (rather than the preferred version of "sin no more"). The Geneva Bible of 1562 reads, "Blessed are the placemakers [peacemakers]" and, according to F. F. Bruce, the so-called Murderers' Bible of 1795 has the line: "Let the children first be killed [filled]." According to *The Christian Writer's Manual of Style* (edited by Robert Hudson) a "1611 King James version [Bible] has Judas rather than Jesus initiating the Last Supper." Finally, in a 1702 Bible, King David laments that "Printers [Princes] have persecuted me without cause." They obviously made a habit of it.

SAINT PAUL WAS A TENT-MAKER

CHRISTIAN CONVERT PAUL OF TARSUS WAS BORN AROUND 10 A.D. The *Encyclopaedia Britannica* points out that although Paul "never met Jesus," he authored the earliest Christian writing. Fourteen of the New Testament books are attributed to him. In them he offers instruction and admonishment, and through them he helped Christianity grow from a small sect into a major religion. It is surprising, then, to learn that Saint Paul was a manual worker: a tent-maker.

From Acts we learn that Paul visited an acquaintance in Corinth "and because he was a tent-maker as they were, he stayed and worked with them." Writing in *St. Paul's Corinth*, Jerome Murphy-O'Connor confirms that "there is no doubt that Paul supported himself by manual labor whilst ministering in Corinth." The *Encyclopaedia Britannica* agrees: "Like most rabbis, he supported himself with a manual trade—tent-making— probably learned from his father."

Saint Paul preached on the move, which made his choice of trade quite convenient. *The Cambridge Companion to St. Paul* (edited by James D. G. Dunn) explains that "he had to work to support himself." The volume adds that "Paul was forced to do 'bit-work' in the leather or tent-making trade in the tanners' quarters, as he moved from one city to the next."

In I Corinthians, Paul identifies himself with laborers: "We work hard with our own hands. When we are cursed, we bless; when we are persecuted, we endure it; when we are slandered, we answer kindly." It would also appear that Saint Paul, just like many a laborer, felt beleaguered at times, since he goes on to add that "up to this moment we have become the scum of the earth."

SAINT NICHOLAS BEGAN HIS PRESENT-GIVING TRADITION BY BUYING CHILDREN OUT OF PROSTITUTION

LITTLE IS KNOWN OF THE REAL LIFE OF THIS BISHOP OF MYRA IN Turkey, but he is believed to have lived in the fourth century. In *Saints and Feast Days*, Kathleen Glavich points out that the majority of stories describe Saint Nicholas helping the poor. The *Encyclopaedia Britannica* describes one such story where the godly man "was reputed to have given marriage dowries of gold to three girls whom poverty would otherwise have forced into lives of prostitution." Lavinia Cohn-Sherbok, author of *Who's Who in Christianity*, adds the interesting fact that "pawnbrokers commonly work under the sign of three gold balls commemorating those gifts." The tale is the forerunner of modern-day Santa and his present-giving tradition. (Apparently the saint also "restored to life three children who had been chopped up by a butcher and put in a tub of brine," but this tale didn't find its way into our Christmas festivities.)

Brewer's Dictionary of Phrase & Fable explains how, in the surrounding regions, the saint was commemorated on December 6 when someone would dress as a bishop and give small gifts to "good children." *The Oxford Companion to the Year* explains that in the Middle Ages in England, the custom was to elect "a boy bishop on this day." In *Remainse of Gentilisme and Judaisme*, seventeenth-century writer John Aubrey describes a jolly commemoration of Saint Nicholas at a school in a church in Yeovil, Somerset, where "they have annually at that time a Barrell of good Ale brought into the church; and that night they [the Schoole-boies] have the priviledge to breake open their Masters Cellar-dore."

Sixteenth-century Dutch colonists took the tradition of Saint Nicholas to America. *Cassell's Dictionary of Word Histories* explains that the Dutch dialect name Sante Klaas became "Santa Claus."

During the middle of the nineteenth century, the German toys-under-the-Christmas-tree tradition caught on in Britain and the U.S. and the festivities shifted from early December to Christmas Day. However, many people in the European Low Countries continue to commemorate Saint Nicholas's generosity by leaving gifts for children on the eve of December 5th.

THE ORIGINAL VERSION OF SAINT MARK'S GOSPEL HAD NO ACCOUNT OF THE RESURRECTION

MARK'S GOSPEL IS THE SECOND NEW TESTAMENT NARRATIVE recounting the life of Jesus Christ. It's thought to have been written by John Mark, who was believed to have been a disciple of Peter the apostle and an associate of Paul of Tarsus. The *Encyclopaedia Britannica* adds that "most scholars agree that it [Mark's Gospel] was used by Matthew and Luke in composing their accounts."

In Mark's Gospel, the final passage "is omitted in some manuscripts, including the two oldest." In these very first Bibles, Mark's Gospel ends, "Trembling and bewildered, the women went out and fled from the tomb. They said nothing to anyone, because they were afraid." *The New Oxford Annotated Bible with the Apocrypha* (edited by Michael D. Coogan) points out that "there was apparently no resurrection appearance in the original text of Mark." Professor of New Testament studies Eugene LaVerdiere, writing in *The Beginning of the Gospel*, describes this as "a very striking and extremely challenging conclusion."

Britannica claims that "many scholars believe that these last verses were not written by Mark, at least not at the same time as the balance of the Gospel." *The Oxford Bible Commentary*, edited by John Barton and John Muddiman, states that "by universal consent, the sequel as we have it comprises only verses 1–8 of this chapter." The volume adds that follow-up verses are "clearly not by the author," explaining that the rest of the gospel "represents attempts to complete the narrative." James R. Edwards, author of *The Gospel According to Mark*, sug-

gests that the final chapter may have been lost or Mark may have died before completing it. However, Dr. W. R. Telford, writing in *The Theology of the Gospel of Mark*, states that "the majority of scholars would now hold that 16:8 was the original ending of the Gospel, and this judgment has been reinforced by recent literary studies."

The practice of adding bits on to the end of existing texts wasn't unique to Mark's Gospel. The final chapter of John's Gospel, according to *Britannica*, also "appears to be a later addition." The assertion that "this is the disciple who testifieth of these things, and wrote these things, and we know that his testimony is true" certainly reads like an addition to the original text.

LaVerdiere suggests that the ending of Mark "was clearly not part of the original Gospel according to Mark." He goes on to suggest that "nor did Mark, the author of 'the beginning of the Gospel,' add it later." LaVerdiere feels that "the consensus of scholarly opinion is that Mark both intended and actually did end the Gospel with the flight of the women." *Britannica* points out that many scholars believe the follow-up verses were "added later to account for the Resurrection." LaVerdiere proposes that this addition "was written and appended to Mark sometime in the second century, when the four Gospels were collected."

THE PURITANS BANNED CHRISTMAS (AND OTHER FORMS OF ENJOYMENT)

ELIZABETHAN PURITAN PHILIP STUBBES, WRITING IN HIS 1583 pamphlet *Anatomie of Abuses*, describes the Christmas pageant "The Lord of Misrule" as follows: "Then march these heathen company towards the church and church yard, their pipers piping, drummers thundering... their bells jingling, their handkerchiefs swinging about their heads like madmen, their hobby horses and other monsters skirmishing amongst the throng: and in this sort they go to the church (though the minister be at prayer or preaching) dancing and swinging their handkerchiefs over their heads, in the church, like devils incarnate." Clearly, it was thought by this particular observer that seventeenth-century folk were having too good a time on their way to devotion.

In *Histriomastix*, written in 1633, English Puritan William Prynne stated that Christmas should be "a day of mourning [rather] than rejoicing," and not spent in "amorous mixt, voluptuous, unchristian, that I say not pagan, dancing, to gods, Christ's dishonour, religion's scandal, chastities' shipwracke and sinnes' advantage." The revelry had to stop. Puritans of the Massachusetts Bay Colony in the

newly settled America were of the same mind. Penne L. Restad, writing in *Christmas in America*, reveals that Governor John Winthrop "entered nothing in his diary on his first Christmas in America in 1630," and in succeeding years "he attempted to suppress the holiday."

Meanwhile, in England the Protestant "godly" or parliamentary party set about putting an end not just to dancing, but to Christmas and other religious festivals. First of all, the party took the Catholic-sounding "mass" out of "Christmas" and changed it into "Christ-tide." Restad reveals that the British Parliament "ordered that the monthly fast, which coincidentally fell on Christmas in 1644, be kept." In 1647, Parliament passed an ordinance abolishing feasts at Christmas, Easter, and Whitsun. The second Tuesday of the month was provided as a secular holiday for workers. He also tells us that "Ministers who preached on the Nativity risked imprisonment" and churchwardens who decorated their churches "faced fines." Restad describes how Londoners who "decorated churches and shops" were forced to watch the Lord Mayor and his marshal ride round "setting fire to their handiwork."

As for Christmas itself, in 1652 Parliament "strongly prohibited" its observance. Lord Protector Oliver Cromwell didn't personally ban Christmas, since these measures were already in force when he came to power the following year, but no doubt he supported the legislation.

Seventeenth-century English lawyer Sir Bulstrode Whitelocke, writing in *Memorials of English Affairs*, stated that in Canterbury, when the Lord Mayor ordered the markets kept open on Christmas Day "serious disturbance ensued... wherein many were severely hurt." He adds that the shopkeepers who obeyed the law were "so roughly used" that they were obliged to petition Parliament for protection. In *Righte Merrie Christmas*, John

Ashton quotes a Member of Parliament lamenting that "these poor simple creatures are mad after superstitious festivals."

In 1658, Cromwell died, and with him the aspirations of the Commonwealth. Two years later Charles II was invited to reclaim the British throne. The monarchy was restored, and so was Christmas.

IN THE OLD TESTAMENT, THE BOOK OF ESTHER AND THE SONG OF SOLOMON DO NOT CONTAIN THE WORD "GOD"

THE OLD TESTAMENT IS MADE UP OF A NUMBER OF BOOKS. THE FIRST six, the Hexateuch, narrate how the Israelites became a people and settled in the Promised Land. The following seven continue their story in the Promised Land, describing the establishment and development of the monarchy and the messages of the prophets. The last eleven books contain poetry, theology, and some additional historical works. The Book of Esther is included in this latter category, and according to the *Encyclopaedia Britannica* it gives an explanation of "how the feast of Purim came to be celebrated by the Jews." *Britannica* confirms that "the divine name is never mentioned" throughout this book.

Britannica also suggests that the book's "secular character... made its admission into the biblical canon highly questionable for both Jews and Christians." In an attempt to remedy this, "the redactors [editors] of its Greek translation... interspersed many additional verses... that demonstrated Esther's... religious devotion." These verses don't appear in the actual text of many Bibles specifically because they are later additions.

The Song of Solomon also comes from the third portion of the Old Testament and neither does God get a mention here. In the past it has been variously interpreted as an allegory for God's love for the Israelites, Christ's love for His Church, or Christ's love for the human soul. *Britannica* suggests an interpretation that has "gained the most credence among modern scholars": that it is simply "a collection of secular love poems without any religious implications." Indeed, *The International Standard Bible Encyclopedia* (edited by Geoffrey W. Bromiley) suggests that "the book's place in the Scriptures frustrates any attempt to denigrate the sensual aspect of human life." (Try telling that to the Puritans.)

CHAPTER 15

Laws *and* Customs

IN NINETEENTH-CENTURY ENGLAND, WIVES WERE SOLD AT MARKET

READERS FAMILIAR WITH THOMAS HARDY'S 1886 NOVEL *THE MAYOR of Casterbridge* will recall how Michael Henchard, in a state of rum-induced drunkenness, auctions Susan, his wife, and their baby daughter for the sum of five guineas. In the preface to the book, Hardy explains that events were based on incidences "in the real history of the town called Casterbridge [Dorchester, England] and the neighboring county." Christine Winfield's essay "Factual Sources of Two Episodes in *The Mayor of Casterbridge*," which is included in *Nineteenth-Century Fiction* (Volume 25, 1970), points out that Hardy, once a magistrate, had collected details of three such "wife sales" dating from the 1820s. Hardy's notes describe how a Brighton man auctioned a "tidy-looking woman" with a "halter round her neck" for thirty shillings. (The winner was charged an extra shilling by the husband for his work as auctioneer.)

The *Annual Register of 1832* (a contemporary news roundup) records how Carlisle farmer Joseph Thomson auctioned his wife Mary Anne. The *Register* describes her as a "spruce and lively damsel, apparently not exceeding twenty-two years of age," and points out that the parting was "by mutual agreement." Thomson asked fifty shillings for her, but only grossed twenty since he described Mary Anne as a "nightly invasion and a daily devil"— clearly, he needed to brush up on his selling technique. Thomson did add, however, that she also had a "sunny side," explaining that she could "read novels and milk cows." After "an hour or two" Mary Anne was finally purchased by "pensioner" Henry Mears. Thomson persuaded Mears to throw in his Newfoundland dog, to which he attached the halter "which his wife had taken off," and proceeded "to the first public house, where he spent the remainder of the day."

The right to sell one's wife was at no point legal under English law, as Hartley Thompson of Little Horton near Bradford found out to his cost in 1858. Victorian reference book writer Robert Chambers, in his *Book of Days* (Part 2), records Thompson's sentence set at "one month's imprisonment and hard labor for selling or attempting to sell his wife." While wife-selling was a rare occurrence, indeed rare enough to draw a crowd, Chambers explains that during the nineteenth century, "this right [was] believed in more extensively than we are apt to imagine." So it would appear.

IN VICTORIAN ENGLAND THE AGE OF CONSENT WAS TWELVE

MANY PEOPLE SEE THE VICTORIAN ERA AS A GOLDEN TIME OF IMPECcable moral values. However, in *Making Sense of Sexual Consent* (edited by Mark Cowling and Paul Reynolds), we learn that "the 'age of consent' for sexual behavior between a male and female was legally codified at the age of twelve by the Offences Against the Person Act 1861 in England, Wales and Ireland." Likewise, the minimum marriageable age for a girl was also twelve. Even more surprisingly, history lecturer Elizabeth A. Foyster's essay  "Silent Witnesses?" included in *Childhood in Question* (edited by Anthony Fletcher and Stephen Hussey), reveals that "although legally the age of consent in the eighteenth century was twelve," a previous "1576 Act had made any sexual intercourse with a child below the age of ten a felony." This meant that "if the girl was between the age of ten and twelve then sexual intercourse only constituted a misdemeanour and non-consent had to be proved for the charge of rape." Effectively, this lowered the age of consent to ten.

Needless to say, as *Shaw and History*, edited by Gale K. Larson, points out, this situation made for "traffic in teenage prostitution" since, on the Continent, the age of consent was set at a rather more conservative "twenty-one years of age." The Victorian British government investigated the trafficking to countries such as Belgium, Holland, and France, but dismissed claims that the women concerned were "innocent of any knowledge as to their fate, or entirely unwilling." One investigator is quoted as reporting to Parliament that prostitution was simply "an accepted fact of lower-class life, a sort of family tradition handed down from mother to daughter." Despite this wildly misguided view, *Making Sense of Sexual Consent* goes on to state that the age of consent was "then raised to thirteen by the Offences Against The Person Act 1875."

Not surprisingly, the trafficking continued. Ten years later, enterprising newspaper editor William Stead "arranged to procure a thirteen-year-old girl, Eliza Armstrong, from her mother, ostensibly for the purpose of reselling her abroad as a prostitute." Stead published his report in the *Pall Mall Gazette* in articles entitled "Maiden Tribute of Modern Babylon." Eliza was "kept safe in France...and then returned to her parents after the stunt, but since Stead had neglected to gain the consent of Eliza's father, the editor was sentenced to three months' imprisonment. (Stead later died on the *Titanic*: He sat quietly reading a book in the First-Class Smoking Room while the ship sank.)

The public furor caused by Stead's articles prompted new legislation, and the legal age of consent was raised to sixteen by the Criminal Law Amendment Act 1885. However, the minimum legal age for marriage remained at twelve until 1929, when former Lord Chancellor Lord Buckmaster pointed out, somewhat belatedly, that male miscreants could still evade the law by persuading their young victims to marry them.

In *Delinquent Daughters*, history professor Mary E. Odem reveals that Stead's exposé caused indignation in America—until it was discovered by Women's Christian Temperance Union member Georgia Mark that "in most states the age of consent was ten...and in the state of Delaware the age was only seven." Ruth C. Engs, author of *The Progressive Era's Health Reform Movement*, confirms that in America "until 1885, under common law, the age of consent was ten in over half the states; in Delaware it was seven."

Negotiating Power in Early Modern Society (edited by Michael J. Braddick and John Walter) reveals that "as a result of public pressure, many states between 1887 and 1893 raised their age of consent from ten to at least fourteen years of age." The volume adds that in 1889, Congress "passed legislation raising the age from ten to sixteen years in Washington, DC." Odem confirms this, explaining that the Californian Women's Christian Temperance Union lobbied legislators until, in California in 1889, "legislature raised the age of consent to fourteen." They continued to lobby until "state lawmakers voted in 1897 to raise the age of consent to sixteen." Odem adds that "within ten years the campaign had spread to all regions of the country, achieving impressive legislative changes." Currently, throughout the U.S. the age of consent ranges between sixteen and eighteen years of age.

So much for "Victorian" values.

TEXAS IS LEGALLY ENTITLED TO DIVIDE ITSELF INTO FIVE STATES

BETWEEN 1836 AND 1845, TEXAS WAS A REPUBLIC. HOWEVER, AS FAR back as 1836 the Texan people had, as the *Encyclopaedia Britannica* explains, "voted for annexation by the United States." This finally occurred in 1845, and in *Contemporary American Federalism,* Joseph Francis Zimmerman quotes the joint resolution (5 Stat. 797) of the Congress annexing Texas and authorizing the creation of "new States, of convenient size, not exceeding four in number, in addition to the said State of Texas."

The Texas State Library and Archives Commission confirms that this resolution "provided that Texas could be divided into as many as five states." As the resolution explains, "states...formed out of the territory lying south of thirty-six degrees thirty minutes north latitude, com-  monly known as the Missouri Compromise Line, shall be admitted into the Union, with or without slavery, as the people of each State asking admission shall desire." Conversely, in "states...

formed...north of said Missouri Compromise Line, slavery, or involuntary servitude (except for crime) shall be prohibited." Or as the Commission puts it, "a popular vote would determine whether slavery could exist."

In any event, Texas did not subdivide, and as the Commission states, "although in theory Texas could still be divided into multiple states, any possibility of carving additional states from Texas ended when the Civil War settled the question of slavery once and for all."

It is sometimes claimed that the 1845 resolution also granted Texas the right to withdraw from the United States if it so chose. This part appears to be pure myth. The Commission sets the record straight, stating that "Texas received no special terms in its admission to the Union." It adds that "once Texas had agreed to join the Union, she never had the legal option of leaving, either before or after the Civil War."

A CITIZEN'S ARREST IS LEGAL

A CITIZEN'S ARREST IS AN ARREST MADE BY A MEMBER OF THE public. It dates back to medieval times when, under English common law, sheriffs encouraged citizens to help apprehend miscreants. In *Criminal Procedure*, professor of criminal justice Ronaldo V. Del Carmen tells us that "common law authorizes a citizen's arrest" provided that "a felony has been committed... [and that] the citizen has probable cause to believe that the person arrested committed the crime." However, Del Carmen warns that citizens who make arrests are exposed to prosecution "for false imprisonment" if they get it wrong.

Citizen's arrests are also legal in England, Scotland, France, Canada, Sweden, Australia, New Zealand, and Germany, but as

John Fernie points out, the "power to arrest is slightly different in each" country. Most villains must be caught in the act. Citizen's arrests may well be recognized by law, but they are not recommended by the authorities: The received wisdom is that it's generally best to leave it to the professionals.

IN SOME COUNTRIES IT IS POLITE TO BURP AFTER DINING

BURPING IS A FAVORITE TOPIC WITH SMALL CHILDREN, AND SO THEY will be delighted to learn that this oft-repeated legend is true. Kitty Morse, quoted in *The New American Chef*, points out that one shouldn't be surprised "if you go out to a Moroccan restaurant and hear someone belch." According to Morse, "at the end of the meal, it is polite to burp" because it shows that "you enjoyed the meal." In *The Global Etiquette Guide to Africa and the Middle East*, Dean Foster agrees. When one has finished eating "it is polite to make a slight burp to indicate satisfaction." And the authors of *The Lonely Planet Guide to Morocco* also offer sage advice when visiting the country: "Do slurp your tea or belch to show your appreciation of the fine cooking."

Richard D. Lewis, writing in *When Cultures Collide*, advises that "in Fiji…it is polite (even mandatory) to belch or burp after completing your meal, to show appreciation." Equally, in *The Traveler's Guide to Asian Customs and Manners*, Elizabeth Divine explains that in Malaysia and Singapore "a burp signals appreciation of the food." Richard Stirling, in his work *How to Eat Around the World*, reveals that in Nepal, "it is not only polite, but eminently desirable, to burp—yes, loudly and grandly—after a meal." In fact, by doing this, "your burp assures the host that you indeed enjoyed your food."

So, next time you witness high-spirited children burping at the table, point out that they would be the very model of good manners were they in Morocco or Nepal, and congratulate them on their sound knowledge of global etiquette. If this doesn't deter them from repeating the offense in future, it will at least confuse them into a moment of burp-free silence.

YOU MUST NOT SMILE IN A PASSPORT PHOTO

THIS INSTRUCTION SOUNDS LIKE A RELIC FROM THE DAYS of authoritarian bureaucracy, but these days it's even more 'important to keep a straight face in your passport photograph. Modern computerized facial recognition systems work by matching up key areas on the subject's face. They only work well when features are uniform.

The State Department's Passport Services Office provides the following guidelines: "The subject's expression should be neutral (non-smiling) with both eyes open, and mouth closed. You may smile with a closed jaw (mouth)...but this is not preferred." When posing for your passport photos, a smile is most definitely frowned upon by the powers that be.

IN PARTS OF EUROPE, A NOD MEANS "NO" AND A SHAKE OF THE HEAD MEANS "YES"

MOST PEOPLE WOULD ARGUE THAT NODDING FOR "YES" AND SHAKING the head for "no" are globally recognized gestures. However, nineteenth-century naturalist Charles Darwin pointed out in *The Expression of the Emotions in Man and Animals* that "the throwing back of the head with a cluck of the tongue is said to be used as a negative by the...Greeks and Turks." (This appears to be describing a no-and-be-off-with-you head gesture.) A modern guide to business-greeting protocol, *Kiss, Bow, or Shake Hands* (by Morrison, Conaway, and Borden), confirms what Darwin suggested, describing the Greek "upward nod of the head" as indicating "no," and explaining that in Turkey a headshake means "I don't understand."

Paul Greenway, in his book *Bulgaria*, explains that natives of the country also "nod their head to mean 'no.'" According to Greenway, Bulgarians "shake their head in a curved, almost bouncy motion to indicate 'yes,'" In *Kiss, Bow, or Shake Hands*, the Turkish are described as tilting their heads from side to side to indicate "yes."

To add to the confusion, Greenway warns that well-traveled Bulgarians, in an attempt to "help" puzzled foreigners, "may do the opposite." Baffled and bewildered? Why not stay home and avoid all this unnecessary confusion?

CHAPTER 16

Quotes *and* Sayings

"WITH GREAT POWER THERE MUST ALSO COME GREAT RESPONSIBILITY" ORIGINATED IN A *SPIDER-MAN* COMIC

MANY GREAT LEADERS HAVE ATTEMPTED TO ORIGINATE MEMO-rable quotes involving the concepts of power in relation to responsibility. British wartime Prime Minister Winston Churchill said, "The price of greatness is responsibility." U.S. President Theodore Roosevelt said, "Responsibility should go with power."

But nobody said it as succinctly as the narrator in the *Spider-Man* comic strip. The quote was penned by Stan Lee in Issue 15 of the 1962 U.S. comic *Amazing Fantasy*, which introduced the action hero (illustrated by Steve Ditko). The strip concluded, "And a lean, silent figure slowly fades into the gathering darkness, aware at last that in this world, with great power there must also come—great responsibility!"

Authors of *A Necessary Fantasy?* Dudley Jones and Tony Watkins claim that the comic-book line has "acquired an almost proverbial resonance."

PRESIDENT GEORGE WASHINGTON'S FAVORITE SAYING, "MANY MICKLES MAKE A MUCKLE," IS GIBBERISH

WRITING IN 1793, GEORGE WASHINGTON pointed out that "there is no adage more true than an old Scotch one, that 'many mickles make a muckle.'" I felt sure that, when I looked up this old and venerated proverb—which had crossed the Atlantic—and translated it from dialect, it would impart some impressive wisdom. But it's utter gibberish.

The *Oxford English Dictionary* confirms that the phrase "Many a mickle makes a muckle" dates back to 1793 and arises from "a misapprehension that... mickle and muckle have opposite meanings, the former representing 'a small amount' and the latter 'a large amount.'" The *OED* corrects this misapprehension, explaining that "mickle" and "muckle" are "variants of the same word," which means "much."

The *Oxford Library of Words and Phrases* describes the adage as "nonsensical," since "muckle is merely a variant of the dialectical mickle, 'a large quantity or amount.'" Washington's saying, therefore, can be translated as: "A large amount makes a large amount." It's true, in a sense, but not very enlightening.

By quoting this saying, Washington was attempting to convey the idea that problems which "though individually may be trifling, are not found so in the aggregate." In other words, small things add up to something larger. *The Oxford Library of Words and Phrases* gives us the correct version, as used in the nineteenth century by Scottish essayist and historian Thomas Carlyle— "Many a little makes a mickle." Still none the wiser? "Mickle" means "a lot," so Carlyle is saying many small things amount to a lot. Precisely Washington's sentiments, until he got his mickles muddled up with his muckles. And who among us has not made the same mistake?

IN THE NINETEENTH CENTURY, ONE LITERALLY HAD A "CHIP" ON ONE'S SHOULDER

THIS WELL-KNOWN PHRASE MEANS BELIEVING ONESELF TO BE disadvantaged. But why "chip," and what's it doing on the person's shoulder?

Needless to say, the chip in question isn't of the potato variety, but refers to a wood chip. The phrase dates back to early nineteenth-century America. *The Oxford English Dictionary; The Real McCoy: A Dictionary of Peculiar English* by Peter Chadlington; and *The American Heritage Dictionary of Idioms* by Christine Ammer all quote *The Long Island Telegraph* of 1830 explaining that "When two churlish boys were determined to fight, a [wood] chip would be placed on the shoulder of one and the other determined to knock it off at his peril."

One of the earliest British uses of the phrase was by English writer W. Somerset Maugham in his 1930 travel book *The Gentleman in the Parlour*: "He was a man with a chip on his shoulder. Everyone seemed in a conspiracy to slight or injure him."

Initially, the expression appears to have meant someone spoiling for a fight, but has now come to mean someone who feels sensitive about a perceived disadvantage, real or imagined, which reminds me of the apocryphal employee reference that goes: "John is a well-balanced individual. He has a chip on *both* shoulders."

RED SKY AT NIGHT, SHEPHERD'S DELIGHT

MUCH WEATHER–PREDICTION FOLKLORE IS NOT TO BE TRUSTED. HOW-ever, my husband has always been impressed by my uncanny ability to predict the following day's weather with a greater accuracy than the forecasters. I use nothing more than the saying "Red sky

at night, shepherd's delight / Red sky at morning, shepherd's warning." It's considered by most experts to be pretty accurate. Meteorologist Dr. Mel Goldstein, writing in the aptly titled *Weather*, confirms that it works, while Elbert S. Mallory, author of *Piloting & Seamanship*, agrees that this is a "reliable proverb."

The proverb is ancient. As indicated in the *Oxford Dictionary of Proverbs* (edited by Jennifer Speake), it is also mentioned in Matthew's Gospel: "When it is evening, ye say, It will be fair weather: for the sky is red. And in the morning, It will be foul weather today, for the sky is red and lowering." Shakespeare also gives it a mention in his poem "Venus and Adonis": "Like a red morn that ever yet betokened / Wreck to the seaman, tempest to the field, / Sorrow to shepherds, woe unto the birds, / Gusts and foul flaws to herdmen and to herds."

The saying is also found elsewhere in Europe: The Italian equivalent is "*Sera rossa e bianco mattino, allegro il pellegrino,*" which translates as "A red evening and a white morning rejoice the pilgrim."

Explanations of how the saying works hinge on the fact that weather, as the United Kingdom Meteorological Office informs us, normally moves "from west to east because our prevailing winds are from the west or southwest." A clear western sky usually indicates good weather to come, but if it's overcast in this region, storms may follow. The sun sets in the west. If we can see the sunset, the chances are that the western sky is cloud-free with a dry atmosphere, and that's the weather we can expect.

Conversely, the opposite is true in the morning. If there is a red tinge to the eastern sky in the morning, this indicates that the fair weather is in the east and has probably passed over. A change for the worse may be on its way.

CHAPTER 17

Truths Proclaimed Wrong That Were Right All Along

The following entries form a collection of falsely discredited facts

NATIVE AMERICAN INDIANS ORIGINATED SCALPING IN THE AMERICAS

BEFORE THE FIRST HALF OF THE TWENTIETH CENTURY, IT WAS TAKEN for granted that Native Americans were in the habit of collecting war trophies from their enemies in the form of sections of scalp. However, during the 1960s this belief was refuted. James Axtell, in his essay "Scalps and Scalping" (included in the *Encyclopedia of North American Indians*), explains that some people argued that "Native Americans had never scalped until they were taught and encouraged to do so by European colonists." The *Encyclopaedia Britannica* reveals that "French, English, Dutch, and Spanish colonial authorities" encouraged the practice by offering bounties "for the scalps of enemy Indians," but the activity was not originated by the Europeans. Axtell claims that the revised version of Native American history suited the rebellious mood of the 1960s and "was quickly adopted by many as conventional wisdom."

Scalping appears to be an ancient practice. In *The Histories*, fifth-century B.C. Greek historian Herodotus records how eighth-century B.C. Scythians would claim their share of war spoils by producing a section of enemy scalp to prove they had played their part in the battle. To obtain this the warrior would make "a circular cut around the head at the ears," remove the skin from the skull, scrape it clean with "a cow's rib," and fasten it to his horse's bridle. The more successful warriors also made themselves "patchwork leather" coats from their trophies.

The prevalence of scalping in America appears to predate the arrival of sixteenth-century European colonists by some time, since Axtell claims that ancient Native American skulls dating back to the sixth century B.C. bear "cuts and scratches just where scalps were traditionally lifted." According to notes in *The Voyages of Jacques Cartier*, the sixteenth-century traveler witnessed the "scalps of five men, stretched on hoops like parchment." Similarly, French expeditionary artist Jacques Le Moyne, in his 1591 observations *Brevis narratio eorum quae in Florida Americai provincia Gallis acciderunt*, noted that "mighty Chief Holata Outina [had] those who were especially employed to carry away the dead during these skirmishes and cut off their enemy's scalps." Le Moyne went on to explain that "with a reed sharper than any steel blade, they cut the skin round the head then, tying the hair a yard in length into a bun, they pulled it off the skull." After the act of scalping had taken place, the scalp was then dried "until it looked like parchment" and the victors "triumphantly displayed [it] on their spear-points." Theodore de Bry's engraving *How Outina's Warriors Dealt with the Enemy's Corpses* graphically depicts Le Moyne's observations (his original illustrations having been destroyed during battle).

As to the purpose of scalping, *Britannica* explains that "for Southeastern Indians it was necessary to take scalps to become a warrior and to placate the spirits of the dead." Although scalps were usually taken from dead enemies, "some Plains Indians preferred a live victim." In such cases "the operation was not necessarily fatal." Indeed, eighteenth-century physician James Robertson's *Remarks on the Management of the Scalped-Head*, which appeared in an early nineteenth-century Philadelphian medical journal, recorded that the wound "cures very slowly" taking about "two years." Presumably, during this somewhat bald period, some kind of hat would have been necessary, for decency's sake.

GLASS IS A SOLID

HOW MANY TIMES HAVE YOU KNOCKED ON THE WINDOW, ONLY TO find your hand passing through the glass pane in the manner of a sci-fi movie? Never. However, back in the 1950s, as art historian Tina Oldknow reveals in *Clearly Inspired*, scientists termed hardened glass "a supercooled liquid, a never-quite-solid amorphous mass." Some caught on to the term, and sought to prove its validity by citing antique windowpanes as proof of this "fact."

A trip to an old cathedral will confirm that ancient glass panes are generally thicker at the bottom than the top. The reason for this is supposedly because the glass has flowed downward over centuries. Corroboration was then found where none existed: It was even claimed that glass manufacturers supplied sheet glass with the instruction "Store flat" so that it didn't start dripping onto the floor. (It was, in reality, to avoid accidents.)

The misconception appears to date back to 1930s German physicist Gustav Tammann, who speculated in his work *Der Glaszusand* that glass was "a frozen super-cooled" liquid. Tammann's theory appears to have been misinterpreted, and, since then, as Sergei V. Nemilov points out in *Thermodynamic and Kinetic Aspects of the Vitreous State*, "a conviction has been established that glass is a kind of supercooled liquid."

Glass is made from silica, soda, and lime heated to a high temperature, which, according to Oldknow, turns into a "disordered molecular structure" similar to that of a liquid. However, Oldknow is quick to add that glass also possesses "a mechanical rigidity, characteristic of crystalline materials." In *Understanding Solids*, Professor Richard J. D. Tilley of Cardiff University states: "Glass is not a liquid, but a solid." Ernst-Joachim Donth, physics professor at the University of Halle in Germany, and author of *The Glass Transition*, confirms this: "The use of 'supercooled liquid' as a synonym for a 'glass-forming substance' is...misleading." The *Encyclopaedia Britannica* states that glass is "an inorganic solid material."

So how do we explain those medieval cathedral glass panes being thicker at the bottom than at the top? In *City of Light*, Jeff Hecht reveals that it's "an artefact of old glass-making techniques," a consequence of which was that they "did not yield flat sheets." *Journal of Chemical Education* contributor Robert C. Plumb explains the "Crown glass process" in a little more detail. The molten glass was "spun in a flashing furnace," resulting in a disc of glass that was thickest at the edge. Plumb points out that "it would certainly make good sense to install the glass with the thick edge down!"

As for the theory of glass "flowing down" over centuries, the research of Edgar D. Zanotto and Prabhat Gupta, included in *The American Journal of Physics* (March 1999, Volume 67, Issue 3, pp. 260–2), concluded that "window glass cannot flow at room temperature in human time scales." Just as well really, otherwise those prized museum displays of Egyptian glass vessels and Roman glass bowls would now be no more than unrecognizable misshapen blobs.

CHOP SUEY AND CHOW MEIN ARE CHINESE DISHES

VARIOUS DIFFERING LEGENDS HAVE IT THAT, AS *THE Oxford Companion to Food* explains, chop suey was invented by "a Chinese cook (usually in California), confronted by a demand for exigent food at an hour when everything on the menu was 'off.'" The cook is then said to have improvised from a mixture of leftovers and called the dish "chop suey," meaning "odds and ends" in Chinese.

The Oxford Companion adds that the identity of the demanding diners varies from drunken miners to a San Francisco political boss, and from railroad workers to a visiting Chinese dignitary. These stories are regularly found online and in print with the general implication that chop suey is a cheap and cheerful dish palmed off on undiscerning Westerners.

Fortunately, *The Oxford Companion* also furnishes us with anthropologist

E. N. Anderson's accurate explanation that chop suey originated from Toisan, "a rural district south of Canton." These Toisan inhabitants were early immigrants to California. Naturally, they prepared food with which they were familiar, and according to Anderson, "chop suey" is an anglicization of the Cantonese *tsap seui* or the Mandarin *tsa sui*, both meaning "miscellaneous scraps." Rhonda Lauret Parkinson, author of *The Everything Chinese Cookbook*, agrees that the dish originated with "Chinese farmers who used to eat a dish of stir-fried vegetables after a long day working in the fields." Just like everyone else, it's logical that Cantonese folk would have a dish based on "whatever comes to hand," and this appears to be it.

Likewise, chow mein is often accused of being a modern faux Chinese dish, yet Parkinson dates the origin of mein (egg noodles) to northern China in the first century B.C. She claims that while Western-style chow mein is designed to appeal to Western tastes, "it is based on an authentic Chinese dish." It's true that carrots and broccoli are not traditional Chinese vegetables but, out of necessity, displaced regional dishes are obliged to include available ingredients.

The Oxford Companion to Food confirms that chow mein takes its name from *chao mian*, a Chinese dish consisting of "previously boiled noodles stir-fried with meat and vegetables." Parkinson suggests that the misapprehension may have arisen because our perceptions of Chinese food were based on early Chinese immigrants, who came primarily from the Canton (Guangzhou) region in southern China: "Since they ate rice, we assumed all Chinese eat rice." However, "wheat and not rice is the staple crop in the north." Parkinson explains that "chow mein refers to the Hong Kong style of pan-frying the noodles in much the same way lo mein refers to the Cantonese style of stir-frying" them.

The Oxford Companion points out that in the Western version of chow mein the noodles are generally deep-fried. It would appear that both chop suey and chow mein have their origins firmly rooted in China, and not only that but they neatly symbolize northern and southern styles of Chinese cooking.

Conversely, Chinese fortune cookies are a wholly American invention.

THERE IS ONE DEFINITIVE LIST OF APOSTLES

WHEN COMPARING THE LISTS OF APOSTLES IN MATTHEW 10, LUKE 6, and Mark 3 (twenty-first-century King James Version), some names are easily recognizable as the same people, yet others do not appear to tally up. The Gospels agree on Simon (Peter) and James and John (the latter two being the sons of Zebedee), followed by Andrew, Philip, and Bartholomew, then Matthew and Thomas (the publican). James the son of Alphaeus is listed by all, as is Judas Iscariot, while Simon the Canaanite is termed "the Zealot" in Luke 6.

This leaves us with a consensus except for the last apostle.

He is Labbaeus (whose surname was Thaddaeus) or Judas, brother/son of James. If Thaddaeus and this Judas are the same person the consensus is complete. There does appear to be some confusion as to the identity of this twelfth apostle: The *Encyclopaedia Britannica* points out that the Greek Orthodox Church distinguishes Judas (Jude) from Thaddaeus. However, it suggests that Saint Judas (generally known as Saint Jude to distinguish him from Judas Iscariot) "is...probably identified with Thaddaeus (Labbaeus)."

One Hundred Saints (based on the Reverend Alban Butler's work) also takes the view that "the apostle Jude (Judas), also called Thaddeus (or Lebbeus)...is usually regarded as the brother of Saint James the Less."

CINDERELLA WORE GLASS SLIPPERS

ONCE UPON A TIME, CINDERELLA'S SLIPPERS WERE MADE OF GLASS— until nineteenth-century French novelist Honoré de Balzac, in his 1841 work *Sur Catherine de Médicis*, explained that the word *vair*, which he defines as "Siberian sable," had become so obsolete that "in a vast number of editions of Perrault's famous tale, Cinderella's slipper, which was no doubt of *vair* (the fur), is said to have been made of *verre* (glass)." The legend then developed that the glass slipper was a mistranslation for fur slipper.

The only problem with this elegant theory is that seventeenth-century French author Charles Perrault's original 1697 tale is titled *Cendrillon, ou la petite pantoufle de verre* (*Cinderella, or the little glass slipper*). Perrault, writing in his native language, must surely have intended the slipper to be glass, since he describes it as such in the title of his tale. In it, "the

Prince took up [Cinderella's lost slipper] most carefully." Would he have been so careful had it been made of fur?

In *The Owl, the Raven, and the Dove*, G. Ronald Murphy explains that Perrault based his work on an earlier Italian folktale called *La Gatta Cenerentola* (*The Cinder Cat*). Cinderella's "slipper flies out of the coach window," but the slipper's appearance isn't further described.

Cinderella-type stories date back to ninth-century China. In *The Classic Fairy Tale*, Iona and Peter Opie recount how Yen-hsien wore "a cloak of kingfisher feathers and shoes of gold" to a festival. Likewise, in a later nineteenth-century German version by the Brothers Grimm, *Aschenputtle* ("Ash-Wallower"), the lost slipper was returned to its original material: "small and dainty and made of gold." In *Literary Blunders* (an excellent read for anyone interested in lexical slipups), Henry Benjamin Wheatley claims that the slipper is almost invariably made of "some rigid material." A rigid gold or glass slipper would more certainly have prevented large uglysister feet from gaining access as opposed to a more accommodating fur one. In *The Folklore of Fairytale*, MacLeod Yearsley suggests that the mistranslation myth may have arisen "merely on account of the tempting similarity of the words *vair*...and *verre*."

That said, I quite like the image of Cinderella tripping down the palace steps swathed in a gown of "gold and silver, all beset with jewels" and wearing a pair of fluffy mules.

The Final Truth

Believe those who are seeking the truth; doubt those who find it.

ANDRÉ GIDE, French author

Select Bibliography

Ayto, John. *Bloomsbury Dictionary of Word Origins*. Bloomsbury, 1990.

Cobham Brewer, E., and Adrian Room, eds. *Brewer's Dictionary of Phrase and Fable*. 15th ed. HarperResource, 1995.

Davidson, Alan. *The Oxford Companion to Food*. Oxford University Press, 1999.

Fowler, H. W. and others. *Concise Oxford English Dictionary*. Oxford University Press, 2003.

Hoad, T. F., ed. *The Concise Oxford Dictionary of Word Origins*. Oxford University Press, 1986.

Karukstis, Kerry K. and Gerald R. Van Hecke. *Chemistry Connections: The Chemical Basis of Everyday Phenomena*. Elsevier Science, 2003.

Room, Adrian. *Cassell's Dictionary of Word Histories*. Cassell, 2000.

Scott, A. F. *Every One A Witness*. White Lion Publishers, 1974.

Wheatley, Henry Benjamin. *Literary Blunders*. Kessinger, 2004.

Wilson, F. P. *The Oxford Dictionary of English Proverbs*. Clarendon Press, Oxford University Press, 1980.

Useful Websites

http://archives.nd.edu/latgramm.htm
⌈Latin Dictionary and Grammar Aid⌉
www.bartleby.com
⌈searchable quotations site⌉
www.biblegateway.com
⌈searchable online Bible⌉
www.britannica.com
⌈*Encyclopaedia Britannica*⌉
http://sources.eb.com
⌈*Encyclopaedia Britannica* Original Sources⌉
www.fordham.edu/halsall/sbook1.html
⌈Internet Medieval Sourcebook⌉
www.literature.org
⌈The Online Literature Library⌉
www.oed.com
⌈*Oxford English Dictionary*⌉
www.ota.ahds.ac.uk
⌈Oxford Text Archive⌉
www.oxfordreference.com/pub/views/home.html
⌈Oxford Reference Online⌉
www.promo.net/pg
⌈Project Gutenberg—electronic books and texts⌉

www.xreferplus.com/info.jsp
  [Xreferplus Online Reference Library]
www.pedantsrevolt.co.uk